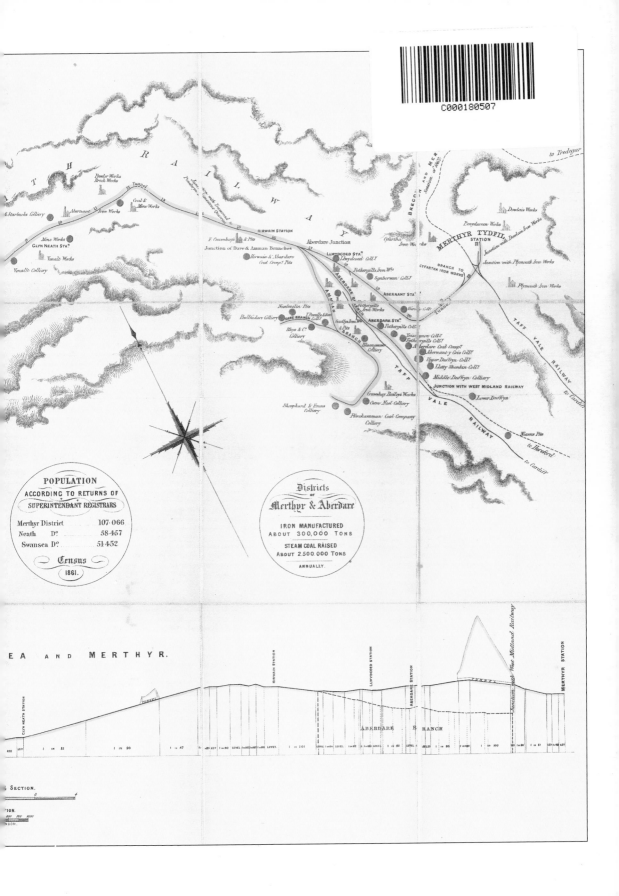

C000180507

RAILWAY

Powder Works Brick Works

Tunnel

Coal & Mine Works

A Starbucks Colliery

Abernant Iron Works

Mine Works

GLYN NEATH STAᴺ

Ynalte Works

Ynalte Colliery

New work freehold Pontydarren sanitine Quarried

HIRWAIN STATION

E Crowshays & Pits

Aberdare Junction

Junction of Dare & Amman Branches

Hirwain & Aberdare Coal Compᵞ Pits

LLWYDCOED STAᴺ

Llwydcoed Colᵞ

Fothergills Iron Wᵏˢ

Cyfartha Iron Works

Signborwen Colᵞ

ABERNANT STAᴺ

Wern Colᵞ

Nantmelin Pits

Bellhadare Colliery

DARE BRANCH Colᵞ

T Powells Colon

Blaze & Cᵒ Colliery

Gadlysplan Nᵒ Pits

Fothergills Iron Works

ABERDARE BᵞCH

BRANCH

ABERDARE STAᴺ

Fothergills Colᵞ

Blaengwa Colliery

Iniwenyowen Colᵞ Fothergills Colᵞˢ

A Aberdare Coal Compᵞ

Abernant y Groin Colᵞ

Upper DuFfryn Colᵞ

Llatty Shordin Colᵞ

Middle DuFfryn Colliery

JUNCTION WITH WEST MIDLAND RAILWAY

Lower DuFfryn

Naeme Pits

Granduy Boileys Works

Ocean Noel Colliery

Sheephard & Evans Colliery

Fforchamman Coal Company Colliery

BRECON AND MER Source of 1809

to Tredegar

Dowlais Works

Penydarren Works

MERTHYR TYDFIL STATION

Junction with Dowlais Iron Works

BRANCH TO CYFARTHA IRON WORKS

Junction with Plymouth Iron Works

Plymouth Iron Works

TAFF VALE RAILWAY to Cardiff

TAFF VALE RAILWAY

to Hereford

to Cardiff

Districts
OF
Merthyr & Aberdare

IRON MANUFACTURED
ABOUT 300,000 TONS

STEAM COAL RAISED
ABOUT 2,500,000 TONS

ANNUALLY.

EA AND MERTHYR.

GLYN NEATH STATION

TUNNEL

HIRWIN STATION

LLWYDCOED STATION

ABERDARE STATION

TUNNEL

Junction with West Midland Railway

MERTHYR STATION

ABERDARE BRANCH

LEV 1 IN 51 1 IN 50 1 IN 47 1 IN 80 LEVEL LEVEL 1 IN 101 LEVEL LEVEL 1 IN 60 LEVEL 1 IN 80 1 IN 400 1 IN 200 LEV 1 IN 51 LEV LEV

SECTION.

TION.
NDON.

THE VALE OF NEATH LINE

(Frontispiece): Quakers Yard Conversation Piece: No. 3717, on the 1.00 p.m. train from Pontypool Road to Neath, taking water at the High Level Station. 5 June 1964.

W. Potter
S. G. Whittaker Collection

THE VALE OF NEATH LINE

from Neath to Pontypool Road

by

Gwyn Briwnant Jones

and

Denis Dunstone

Glyn John A.R.P.S.

First impression—October 1996

ISBN 1 85902 318 5 (Softback)
ISBN 1 85902 446 7 (Hardback)

Printed by
Gomer Press, Llandysul, Ceredigion.

CONTENTS

GW 2-4-0 Metro tank engine with late Victorian carriages contribute to the character of the scene, east of Pencaedrain Tunnel. No date.

WIMM.

FOREWORD

The line treated here falls into two divisions: the Vale of Neath Railway (opened in 1851) running from Neath to Aberdare and Merthyr, and an 1857 extension of the Newport, Abergavenny & Hereford Railway which left a main line from Newport at Pontypool Road and ran westward to meet the Vale of Neath Railway in the Cynon Valley.

The Vale of Neath Railway was built to the broad gauge of 7ft, whereas the extension from Pontypool was constructed to the standard gauge of 4ft-8½ ins. The resulting difficulties were partly overcome by the provision of a third rail, producing a mixed gauge, in 1864, but not fully until the broad gauge was abolished here in 1872. At its southern end the line met the broad-gauge South Wales Railway, providing a connection between Neath and Swansea.

The main business of the whole line was the carriage of coal. The Aberdare coalfield was expanding very rapidly at this time, from 71,000 tons produced in 1844 to 2,343,700 in 1870.

The two largest English railway companies, the London and North Western and the Great Western, fought for the control of the line until the Great Western absorbed it in 1863-6.

The course taken by the Vale of Neath Railway ran through thick woods, with little tributary streams tumbling down the steep hill-sides over innumerable waterfalls. It became a route specially commended to travellers in search of natural beauty. Murray's *Handbook for Travellers in South Wales* paid it careful attention on this account, and the railway reaped useful profits from summer tourist traffic. No comparable history of a British railway company has looked at the passage of the line through the natural landscape with greater care than the authors display in this book, or described it more deftly.

Among the engineering structures on the line there was one great work on the northern section, the Crumlin Viaduct, a landmark in the history of metal bridge-building. Its design and erection are carefully treated here.

Those are the book's chief highlights. But the whole story, as unfolded in it so fully and clearly, forms a useful contribution to the history of the British railway system and to the history of South Wales.

JACK SIMMONS
Leicester

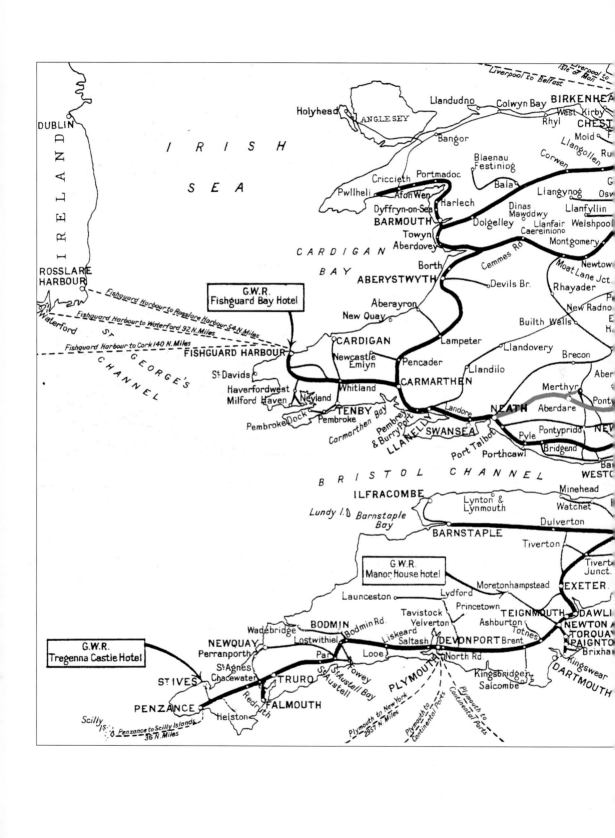

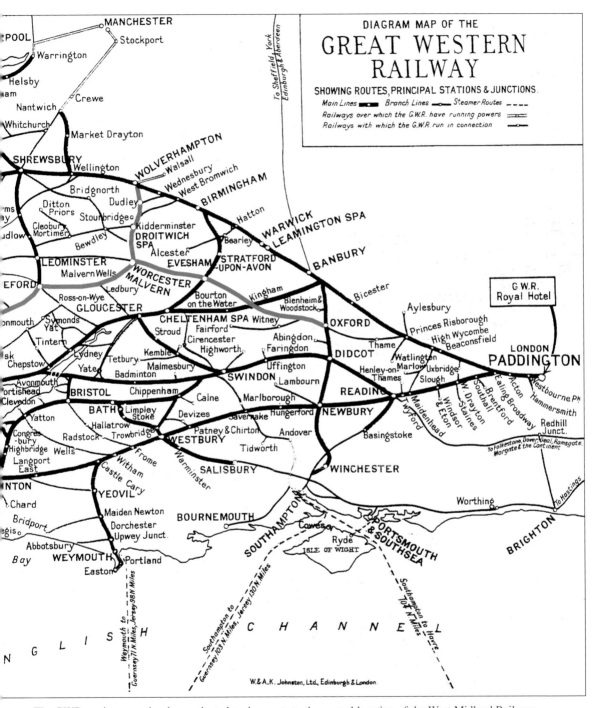

W.&A.K. Johnston, Ltd., Edinburgh & London.

The GWR carriage map has been adapted to demonstrate the central location of the West Midland Railway.
GBJ Collection.

ACKNOWLEDGMENTS

The authors have received much help from contacts made in the course of researching this book and would like to place on record their gratitude. Much of the text is derived from original documents and the professional staff in Museums, Libraries and Record Offices have been most co-operative, from the Public Record Office at Kew, to the House of Lords Record Office, The British Library of Political and Economic Science, the National Library of Wales in Aberystwyth, the Royal Commission on Historical Monuments in Wales, and the County Archives of Mid, South and West Glamorgan and Gwent, the Libraries at Aberdare, Neath, Newport, and Swansea, and the Torfaen Museum at Pontypool and above all, Dr Stuart Owen-Jones, Keeper of the Welsh Industrial and Maritime Museum who, with his staff, has been most supportive and provided ready access to the museum's extensive collection of photographs. In addition private individuals have offered guidance, advice and information; John Mear of Aberdare has been generous with information and advice, as has Bob Grant of Neath, both of whom had carried out research on part of the subject, and Roger Kidner has loaned manuscript material prepared by the late Eric Mountford; Eddie Evans, an expert on the Nelson and Quakers Yard area, has been a most supportive and enthusiastic source of information. Alan Christopher of B.B.C. Wales, F.K. Davies of Neath, Gordon Griffiths of Pontypool, Mr Patterson of Aberdulais, and J.N. Slinn of Woking have also been helpful in a variety of ways.

Most of the illustrations are previously unpublished; individual contributors are credited in the text but the following have been both generous and trusting in lending slides and prints: Gareth Bewes of Bristol, John Davies of Swansea, Wayne Hopkins of Pontllanfraith, Alan Jarvis of Cardiff, R.H. Marrows of Lydney, Gerald Robinson of Maidenhead, J. Stone of Birmingham, W.E. Spurrier, Steve Whittaker of Manchester and Ian Wright of Cambridge. Malcolm James of Rogerstone kindly lent timetables and other ephemera from his extensive collection. The Neath Antiquarian Society also granted access to their interesting collection of maps and contemporary prints and engravings.

Retired railwaymen who remember working the line gave readily of their time to recount some of their experiences, particularly Tony Pook of Nottingham, Howard Jones, Mike Hughes, Rupert Davies, and Marslyn Vater of Aberdare, Bernard Inge of Abergavenny, and Ted Hounslow of Pontypool.

Our final thanks go to Professor Jack Simmons of Leicester for his valuable suggestions and for writing the Foreword.

A charming contemporary portrayal of Pontwalby Viaduct.
Neath Antiquarian Society

Nos. 5222 and 5239 pound their way dramatically up the Glyn Neath bank, presenting a 20th century version of the picturesque.

S. A. Leleux

An atmospheric portrayal of Penrhiwceiber on a wet day..May 1958.

National Monuments Record for Wales.

PREFACE

This book is about a railway but it is also about people, especially the personalities associated with the early days, their management problems and their achievements. Equally it is about places, in particular the Welsh landscape, and the way in which the railway made its way in spite of the obstacles; it is about the structures with which it spanned the valleys and drove through the hills, and about the stations where contact was made with the people who travelled. The railway also picked its way through, over and under a multitude of lesser industrial lines and sidings, and in describing the main line, the authors have resisted the temptation to be drawn down every interesting but intricate by-way. They share an enthusiasm for the railway in the landscape and find that there has been scant acknowledgment of the contribution made by either the industrial landscape or the railway to the generation of the picturesque.

There are several references to the picturesque in this book, and it may therefore be helpful to try to clarify the special sense this word acquired in the second half of the eighteenth century, often in the context of landscape gardening. Inspired by the paintings of Claude Lorraine,

artists sought, both on canvas and when planning country estates, to create scenes which led the eye through experiences of surprise, drama, even horror, to the ideal or romantic; a sunset, a walled city on a distant hill, the far horizon with a departing sailing ship—or quite simply the client's country house. The whole was dominated by a desire to make a scene appear as though created naturally in spite of its deliberate and contrived features. Great names in nineteenth century art from Turner to Monet saw the potential of the railway in the landscape; the authors would argue that a steam train bursting from a tunnel, railway carriages being drawn along a ledge cut in a precipice, or an airy, spindly viaduct bearing a loaded coal train across a steep and wooded valley, all bear comparison as subjects with the follies, grottos, ivy-clad walls and collapsing arches of the conventional picturesque scene.

The Vale of Neath line, as the GWR called the whole line from Neath to Pontypool, though engaged in a dirty and unromantic task, was nevertheless able to enhance and create images arguably as picturesque as many of the contrived scenes of eighteenth century garden designers.

Early engraving of the Pencaedrain Tunnel, south portal.
Neath Antiquarian Society

Sunshine, mist and coal-dust combine in this view of Aberdare.

John Davies.

Llanhilleth churchyard, high above the tide of industry, visited by Coxe in 1799, and little changed since.

DD.

Chapter 1

THE SCENE

That part of south Wales destined to become one of the most intensely industrialised places on earth was originally a sparsely populated, wild and mountainous country which attracted the attention of students of picturesque scenery over many years. When Daniel Defoe arrived in the Taff vale at Merthyr Tydfil he found that place 'most agreeable' and said so in his *Tour of Britain* in 1724. Merthyr, as it is now more generally known, later became the largest centre of iron manufacture in the world, while over the mountain to the south-west in the Cynon valley, the ancient village of Aberdare was to become the centre of the steam coal industry. In 1770, an Anglican parson, William Gilpin, toured the Wye valley and parts of south Wales. He had strong views on what made a landscape picturesque and was struck by the prospect of Neath as his party descended into the Vale of Neath, having crossed the mountains from the north. The celebrated naturalist Alfred Russel Wallace lived for a time in Neath. He wrote in his autobiography that he had seen many of the beautiful places in Britain 'but I cannot call to mind a single valley that in the same extent of country comprises so much beautiful and picturesque scenery, and so many interesting special features as the Vale of Neath'. Another Anglican parson called William Coxe made a tour in 1799 which concentrated on Monmouthshire. From Pontypool he explored westward, to what was then known as 'The Wilds of Monmouthshire', up the Glyn Valley with, on the south side, a precipice formed by the north-eastern flank of Mynydd Maen. The road followed a tramway leading to an iron works situated in the middle of a wood. Coxe was impressed by the wild and romantic scenery.

Neath and Pontypool stand some 40 miles apart at either end of high ground deeply dissected by river valleys; in the west the rivers flow south-west while in the east they run generally south-east, towards the Bristol Channel. The mountains rise to a height just below 2,000ft at a distance of up to 20 miles from the sea. The valleys, often narrow and steep sided, lend themselves to southward communication rather than east-west, and early transport of the coal and iron products moved down the valleys to the coast with the advantage of gravity; passage eastward however, towards England, was less straightforward.

The Ebbw Valley presented a natural barrier to east-west communication.

Alan Jarvis

The junction between the Neath and Tennant Canals at Aberdulais.

WIMM: GW Coll.

A typical canal scene, near Neath, reflecting the later dominance of the railway.

WIMM: GW Coll.

Canal and railway at Aberdulais. 1993

R. H. Marrows

Pontypool like Neath has been involved with industry for centuries. The Hanbury family bought an estate there in 1565 and by 1588 were selling iron smelted in Pontypool. The iron industry was fuelled by charcoal derived from the plentiful supply of trees in the area, but as it took 16 sacks of charcoal to yield 1 ton of pig iron, it is hardly surprising that the iron industry started to decline during the eighteenth century for lack of economically available timber. Fortunately, by around 1760, it was becoming accepted that coke derived from coal provided a satisfactory alternative.

The only route to the sea for the onward distribution of iron products to home or overseas markets lay along the valleys, but the roads were quite inadequate and the rivers unnavigable. Tramways initially provided a solution and had been used for short distances since the seventeenth century. Among the first in Wales

was Sir Thomas Mackworth's of 1695 near Neath; this used wooden rails, though during the eighteenth century iron gradually replaced wood as the material for the rails. However, such tramways had neither the rigidity nor the strength to carry the quantity of traffic which began to develop.

The first viable solution for coping with heavy loads over a distance of up to 20 miles from the new iron works to the sea was the canal. The Neath Canal, linking Glyn Neath to Neath, was authorised by Parliament in 1791, and prospered until 1850. It paid its last dividend in 1896 and finally expired in 1921. The initial need to get iron products from the Cynon valley to the sea was so desperate that until the opening of the Aberdare Canal, trams were hauled by horses westward from Aberdare to the head of the Cynon valley and over the watershed; they were then lowered down a long and steep incline to the Neath canal at the head of the Vale of Neath. An additional outlet was provided by the Tennant Canal which, from a basin at Aberdulais near Neath, enabled cargo to reach the docks at Swansea.

Further east the Monmouthshire Canal Company was smarter (or luckier) than most. The canal from Crumlin to Newport was authorised in 1792, with an arm north from Newport to near Pontypool where it linked with the Brecon & Abergavenny Canal. Under pressure from the ironmasters in 1845 it obtained authorisation from Parliament to build a railway from Newport to Pontypool, and itself to convert tramways to railways. By the time it managed to lease itself to the GWR in 1875, it was effectively a railway company, having altered its name to The Monmouthshire Railway and Canal Company (MRCC) and operating beyond Crumlin to Nantyglo and Ebbw Vale, and from Pontypool to Blaenavon, with branches to collieries along the way.

The Crumlin Viaduct in about 1885 as seen from Crumlin High Level Station.
Cynon Valley Borough Libraries.

Crumlin Valleys Colliery, deep in the Glyn Valley: heavy industry in a sublime environment.
WIMM: GW Coll.

It was the speed and power of the steam engine which rendered the canals largely uncompetitive, and the railways soon evolved to provide the strength and stability of track to support the great weight of the new engines. They also offered the advantage over the canals of significantly less pilferage.

Use of iron stimulated the massive expansion of the economy of south Wales in the period from 1800 to 1850. As iron required coal and transport, and railways in turn needed iron for rails and locomotives, progress spiralled. The early expansion was centred on Merthyr which, during the first three quarters of the nineteenth century, was the largest town in Wales. By 1855 it was four times the size of Cardiff and Newport, with a population of 80,000. In the second half of the century, the demand for iron was largely replaced by steel, which outstripped the availability of Welsh iron ore, so it had to be imported. The decline in the consumption of coal in the iron industry was counteracted by a dramatic increase in demand for a wide number of other purposes. Coal consumption in London, for example, grew thus:

year	'000 tons
1650	216
1750	689
1850	3,639
1938	21,657

The Vale of Neath line curves around Deep Duffryn Colliery. The dumb buffered waggons suggest a date in the nineteenth century.

WIMM: Spencer Powell Coll.

The first significant exports of coal from Cardiff occurred during the 1830s when the Bute West Dock opened in 1839; Newport's new dock followed in 1842. At the same time the first pits were sunk independently of iron works in the Aberdare valley. U.K. and south Wales production grew dramatically and peaked in 1913 at 287 million tons and 57m. respectively. By that time south Wales was producing one third of total world exports. Thereafter, although Welsh production held up well, there was a gradual decline. By 1962 it was down to 17m. tons, mainly for United Kingdom inland consumption.

In terms of British railway history, 1845 was a significant year. By this time, a skeletal national network was already in place; Birmingham was linked to the north-west, to York and Darlington, to London and to Bristol and Exeter. London was linked to Cambridge, Colchester, Dover, Brighton, Gosport and Bristol. In south Wales, Merthyr was linked to Cardiff. It was the year of the Railway Mania in which speculation in new railway shares and applications for Parliamentary approval reached such a level that as many miles of railway were authorised in that year as already existed, namely 2,235 miles (cf. 1994 mileage of 11,000). By 1847, capital investment in railways amounted to 10% of Gross National Product and railway construction employed 250,000 men.

Parliament had inadvertently fuelled the railway investment mania by implying that 10% was an expectable return on the investment in railways. The Railway Act of 1844 provided that the Government might purchase a railway after 21 years if its profits exceeded an average of 10% as Parliament was obsessed by the fear of the railways creating regional monopolies. In practice, a 10% return was rarely achieved and railway returns averaged only 4½%. Profitability

declined as the key indicator, costs expressed as a percentage of receipts, rose from 45% in 1850, to 50% in 1870 and to 63% in 1912.

Many of the projects into which investors rushed were ill-judged and much money was promised which could not be afforded. The average price of railway shares peaked in 1845 and remained high in 1846; collapse came in 1847, prompted by the Irish potato famine and the Repeal of the Corn Laws. Gold reserves were hit by the resulting import of wheat and a coincidental sharp rise in the price of American cotton. The crash caused widespread suffering, many people were ruined, and money became tight.

One of the factors impeding the logical development of the network along purely commercial lines was the existence of two principal gauges. Most of the country was laid to George Stephenson's gauge of 4 ft 8½ ins. In the 1840s this was referred to as the narrow gauge, as the GWR was laid to the broad gauge of

Swansea South Dock ca.1865 demonstrating how mixed-gauge track allowed simultaneous operation of broad- and standard-gauge trains. The broad-gauge train in the centre, featuring flat trucks carrying coal boxes, is hauled by 0-6-0ST No. 19, while the standard-gauge train is in the charge of either No. 24 or No. 25, both delivered from the Vulcan Foundry in March 1865.

WIMM.

7 ft 0¼ ins over the route from London to Bristol. Its allies, operating from Bristol to Gloucester and to Exeter, followed suit. On the other side of the country the Eastern Counties Railway had been laid between London and Colchester to a gauge of 5 ft.

At Gloucester where the broad gauge of the GWR met the narrow gauge from Birmingham, the inconvenience of switching goods and passengers between trains led to many complaints. Accordingly a Parliamentary Committee visited the scene, and were appalled by the confusion and mayhem caused by the need to transfer goods in an inadequate shed. This visit led to the creation of the Gauge Commission which, after lengthy discussion and demonstrations of trains on the broad and narrow gauges, decided in favour of the latter. The Commissioners acknowledged the greater speed and comfort of the broad gauge but were influenced by the comparative mileage of the two systems; 274 laid to the broad gauge and 1,901 miles to the narrow, and considered the fast travel of the few less important than the convenience of general traffic. They shied away from stating that existing broad gauge track should be converted, and confined themselves to making generalisations about the desirability of finding some way for narrow gauge trains to run on broad gauge track. The GWR management launched a lengthy counter-attack. The matter was then referred to the Board of Trade, which felt that it would be an excessive burden to require the GWR to convert at its own expense what had, after all, been sanctioned by Parliament. They also felt it inequitable to charge the other railways for this. It was therefore judged better to leave the existing broad gauge lines in place, and to minimise the problems of interchange for the future by suggesting that only the line from London to Bristol and Exeter, and all lines not yet completed south of this, be broad gauge. This eventually led to The Gauge Act of 1846 which made it unlawful to construct a railway with a gauge other than 4 ft 8½ ins in Great Britain and 5 ft 3 ins in Ireland. Thereafter the former narrow gauge came to be known as standard gauge. However Parliament was not as clear as even the Board of Trade had been,

because it then went on virtually to annul this simple statement by excluding from it any railway in whose enabling act specific provision was made as to gauge. In practice this meant that the burden of proof that a line should not be standard gauge rested on the promoter, but it by no means banned new broad gauge lines.

As a result of the understandable hesitancy of Parliament, the matter remained unclear, though no more broad gauge lines were authorised after 1846 outside the south west of England and south Wales.

At that time, the nearest railhead to south Wales was Gloucester. Wales had been largely by-passed by the first round of railway building and it was principally the urge to speed the mail connection with Ireland which drove the first trunk lines across Wales. As early as 1836 the England and Ireland Union Railway had been projected from Gloucester to Fishguard via Brecon, Llandovery and Carmarthen, but it got nowhere. In 1844 Parliament approved a standard gauge railway from Chester to Holyhead, and a year later, the GWR floated a company to link Gloucester to Fishguard by a railway laid along the Bristol Channel coast. This, the South Wales Railway (SWR), was to be broad gauge and was accepted by Parliament as an exception to the gauge rule.

In the Welsh Marches, Parliament authorised the MRCC in 1845 to build a standard gauge railway from Newport to Pontypool; this was to make Newport a three gauge town (if the 4ft 4ins Western Valley passenger tramway is included). In 1846, it approved the Shrewsbury & Hereford (S&H) and the Newport, Abergavenny & Hereford (NAH), both as standard gauge lines, while in 1848 Shrewsbury was to be linked to Chester by another standard gauge line, thus completing the link along the Border. In approving the S&H, Parliament expressly turned down a simultaneous application to build a broad gauge line from the projected Monmouth & Hereford, to Shrewsbury. The possibility of the frontier between the gauges in Wales being contained on the Bristol Channel coast was lost when the Vale of Neath Railway (VNR) was authorised in 1846 to build a broad gauge line from Neath, on the South Wales Railway, to

Merthyr. So Merthyr, already the terminus of the standard gauge TVR, was to become a two gauge town, followed in 1851 by Aberdare and in 1853 by Hereford.

In 1847 Parliament authorised the NAH to build a standard gauge branch called the Taff Vale Extension Railway (TVE) westward from Pontypool, to link up with the TVR, and thence to have access to Merthyr. No one at that stage saw any advantage in making a link between Neath and Pontypool; Merthyr was the sole objective from both east and west.

This chapter has indicated Welsh railways under construction or authorised along the north and south coasts, down the marches, and to Merthyr; to understand more fully the difficulty for any one scheme to survive, and to give a flavour of the feverish activity associated with railway promotions at this time, it may be helpful to list the railway projects floated during 1845 which had ambitions in Wales. The 'mania' was at its height, the gauge question was still unresolved and there appeared to be plenty of money about. Most of these specific projects failed, though in due course many of the routes envisaged did actually see a railway; the most significant gap, that between Abergavenny, Brecon and Llandovery, was never filled.

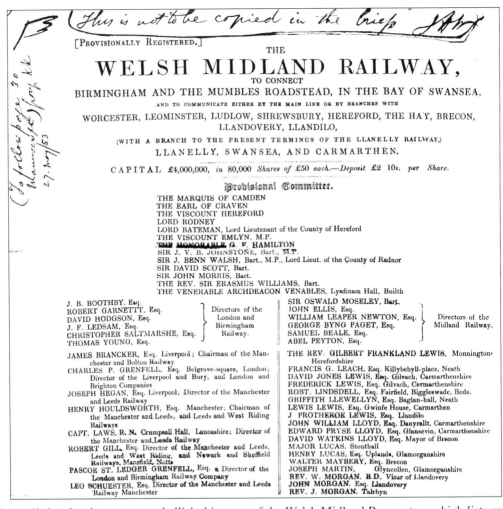

Counsel's hand-written notes embellish this copy of the Welsh Midland Prospectus, which lists some of the august names associated with this dubious venture.

House of Lords Record Office.

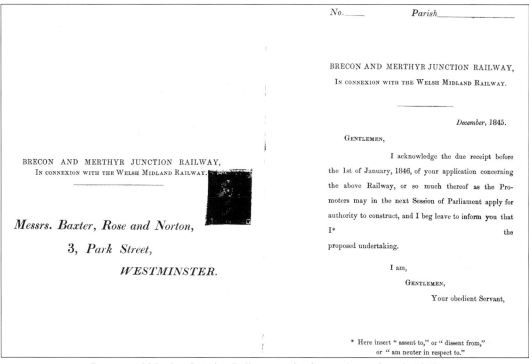

Brecon and Merthyr Junction Railway receipt for purchase of stock, 1845.

GBJ Coll.

Projected Welsh Railway Schemes for 1845.

12 April. The Great Welch (*sic*) Railway, from Carmarthen to Swansea, Brecon, Hereford and Worcester. This bore a close resemblance to:

The Welsh Midland Railway projected from Worcester through Hereford, The Hay (*sic*) and Brecon to Carmarthen, which in May launched a partner branch from Brecon to Merthyr called the Brecon and Merthyr Junction Railway; they were merged in September.

19 April, the Newport, Abergavenny and Hereford.

26 April, the Great Eastern and Western, a really grandiose scheme to build a railway from Yarmouth in Norfolk through Ely, Wisbech, Nuneaton, Birmingham, Worcester, Hereford, Abergavenny, Merthyr, Neath to Swansea. Like some others, they failed to submit their drawings to Parliament on time, due mainly in their case to the gross incompetence and inefficiency of William Gravatt, their Engineer. He was engineer to two other projects which got no further than a set of drawings lodged with the County offices in Monmouth; the Pontypool and Merthyr Tydvil (*sic*) Railway and the Chepstow and Pontypool Railway.

21 May, the Vale of Neath Railway.

23 August, the Great Welsh Junction Railway from Bangor and Porth Dinllaen in north Wales via Caernarfon, Harlech, Dolgellau, Welshpool, Shrewsbury, Hereford, Ross, Monmouth, Merthyr, Neath, Swansea, to Carmarthen.

6 September, the Great North and South Wales and Worcester Railway to run from Carmarthen to Aberystwyth, Machynlleth, and Newtown.

20 September, the Hereford and Merthyr Tydvil (*sic*) Junction Railway, in conjunction with the Gloucester, Aberystwyth and Central Wales Railway. At the same time the Worcester and Merthyr Tydvil (*sic*) Junction Railway was registered to run from Ross to Abergavenny, Nantyglo, and Merthyr.

27 September, the Great Welsh Central Railway, to link Liverpool and Swansea by a straight line which it was ignorantly believed could be drawn through Runcorn, Oswestry, and

Llandovery. This project was to be either with conventional locomotive haulage or by the atmospheric system then being tested in south Devon and south of London. It was one of the most dishonest of the projects, and the accompanying note from the *Railway Times* of 1847 illustrates the risks of railway speculation

and the caution required of investors towards the promotors.

25 October, the Direct Brecon, Abergavenny and Monmouth Independent Junction Railway.

In October 1845 Parliament authorised the Newport and Pontypool Railway.

Since writing the above a circumstance has come to our knowledge which, while it is amusing in its character, is, nevertheless, calculated to give an unfavourable impression as to the manner in which this Company has been conducted. A gentleman who is a considerable shareholder in the concern, who is personally known to us, and in whose veracity we have the utmost confidence, called last week at the offices of the Company to make inquiries as to the position of affairs, and as to the reasons which had led to the announcement which had been made public by the Managing Directors. This gentleman was shown into an elegantly furnished office, and was introduced to an individual of portly appearance, attired in an *outré* style and adorned with a profusion of jewellery, and who was stated to be the Secretary. He was extremely pompous in his demeanour, and in a rather abrupt manner inquired what the gentleman who had been introduced to him required. The gentleman replied that he wished for some information respecting the affairs of the Company. This want however was not destined to be satisfied, as he of the chains and rings said that he was not placed there to answer impertinent questions, or to encourage idle curiosity. The applicant replied, that he was a large shareholder in the concern and had a right to demand an answer to his inquiries, as he wished to obtain such information as would enable him to judge for himself whether the Great Welsh Central Railway Company was a *bona fide* scheme or a bubble. Upon this " the jewelled darling" threw himself into a towering passion, and walking up to the applicant in a threatening and somewhat of a fighting-cock attitude, demanded to know " how a fellow of his appearance dare put such questions to a respectable man respecting a respectable Company." Our informant was taken slightly by surprise by such an attack, and replied that he was not aware that he was bound to study the taste of any one but himself with regard to the matter of his own dress. He further informed the

man with the figured waistcoat that he might rely upon it that he should on the first occasion bring the matter before the shareholders, in order that he might ascertain whether they would countenance such an attack as that which had been made upon him by one of his own servants.

We know that the facts of this case are true —we know that such a scene as that which we have described took place, and we put the matter to the whole body of the shareholders of this Great Welsh Central Railway, and ask them whether they will tolerate such conduct in one of their own officials?

We never had a very high opinion of this Great Welsh Central Railway. It always appeared to us a paper line. It was too good ever to be carried out. Let our readers picture to themselves a railway running right across the principality of Wales in a perfectly straight line, without a single curve of any sort, and let them consider whether such a line ever could be carried out. The line upon the map is one that has been produced by a pen and a ruler.

We will conclude by putting two or three questions to the Managing Directors.

Have the Directors paid upon the shares that were allotted to them ?

Has a single survey ever been made ?

Has any person, authorised by the Company, ever gone over the line of country proposed to be taken ?

Have, in fact, any steps whatever been taken to advance the Company ?

These are questions to which the shareholders would do well to demand immediate answers.

Extract from the *Railway Times*, 1847.
The British Library of Political and Economic Science.

Chapter 2

THE BROAD GAUGE

Key VNR Personnel:

Viscount Villiers	Chairman
I.K. Brunel	Engineer
Admiral Warde	Director
Fred Saunders	Secretary
Joshua Williams	Secretary, later Superintendent
Henry Bruce, 1st Lord Aberdare.	Director, later Chairman
Nash Vaughan	Director, later Chairman
Richard Potter	Chairman GWR

The idea of a railway up the picturesque valley of the river Neath was received with fear and trembling by some of the older inhabitants of the area. One old man feared that the cows would stop giving milk and that the calves would die, while the landlord of The Plough at Abertwrch was afraid that the smoke from passing locomotives would kill his horses.

The Vale of Neath Railway was the brain-child of a local man, H.S. Coke, a solicitor, who was Town Clerk of Neath. On 21 May 1845, he submitted to a meeting in London of the Directors of the South Wales Railway a proposal to build a railway up the Vale of Neath to Merthyr. This was to leave the SWR line at Neath and proceed up the east side of the broad, flat and mainly pastoral valley of the Neath river as far as Glyn Neath; at this point it would begin to climb the side of the steepening hills, pass through a tunnel near the summit and cross the watershed to the Cynon valley. The railway was then to make its way along the hillside to a point above Cwmbach, where it turned and penetrated the Aberdare mountain, emerging on a short decline to a terminus in the heart of Merthyr. A branch to Aberdare was envisaged from the outset.

The broad-gauge VNR approach to the original South Wales Railway bridge at Neath.

WIMM.

Early engraving of VNR train approaching Neath.

Neath Antiquarian Society.

A route across a watershed was hardly desirable for a mineral railway. The climb from Glyn Neath was about 4 miles at a gradient of some 1 in 50, while eastward from the summit near Hirwaun down to Aberdare lay a further 2 miles at 1 in 50. The original intention was to use stationary engines, but the increasing power of locomotives enabled this to be avoided. Nevertheless these gradients remained a problem, especially for trains without continuous brakes, for the life of the line.

The SWR directors agreed to support the plan provided they got their own Parliamentary Act which was then being processed, and provided the landowners agreed; they also required it to be laid out to the broad gauge. A prospectus was prepared and submitted to another SWR meeting on 26 July at which I.K. Brunel was present; it was approved. A so-called Provisional Committee of the VNR met for the first time on 11 August at the SWR London office, 449 West Strand, under the chairmanship of the Earl of Jersey, and resolved to proceed with Brunel as engineer and Fred Saunders (nephew of the GWR Secretary) as secretary. From the outset the style of the VNR was flavoured by Paddington, the SWR itself being a dependant of the GWR.

On 8 November the VNR decided to agree to co-operate with the Great Eastern & Western Railway (GE&W) in their plans to get Parliamentary approval for a broad gauge railway from Hereford to Abergavenny, Nantyglo, and Merthyr, with an extension to the VNR at Hirwaun. They accordingly decided to oppose a scheme of the Welsh Midland Railway (WMR) to build a standard gauge railway from Worcester to Carmarthen in co-operation with the NAH.

At the Parliamentary hearings much evidence was called; a grocer from Merthyr described how food from west Wales was transported by cart, taking a week and costing £5 14s. 0d. per ton; by rail it was expected to cost 12s.. The former proprietor of the Castle Hotel Merthyr described the road from Merthyr to Swansea as the worst he knew in the kingdom. Yet 10 horse-drawn vans each carrying 10 to 15 people made the journey to Swansea every day to go bathing in the sea. Asked why they could not go down to Cardiff by train on the TVR, they replied that it was too muddy there for bathing. Another Merthyr resident produced the surprising evidence that people in Merthyr often ran short of domestic coal.

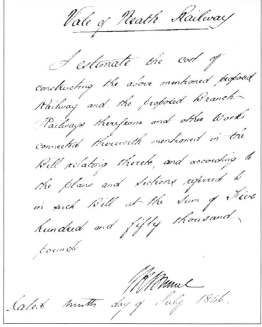

Brunel's confirmation to Parliament of his estimate of the cost of the VNR.

House of Lords Record Office.

The seal of the Vale of Neath Railway.
WIMM: GW Coll.

Under rigorous questioning from counsel for the Tennant canal, Brunel argued that the proposed broad gauge would allow heavier and therefore more powerful engines. As a non-Welshman he was heavily tested on his knowledge of the geography of the Vale of Neath; part of his defence was that he had personally surveyed the route of a road up the valley some years previously. Parliamentary Committees took a particular interest in the gradients on railways, and those on the VNR were accordingly a subject of some discussion and, indeed, amazement to Brunel's contemporaries. A contributor to *Herapath's Journal* stated, 'We have before us one of the most extraordinary productions for a railway which ever passed a committee of the House of Commons. Of all the sections which I have ever seen, I never saw one with such gradients for mineral traffic. Had the line been laid out by anyone but Brunel it would have done for him . . . Mr Robert Stephenson and others were called by the TVR and all spoke in the most decided manner that the line would be dangerous to the public travelling, and enormously expensive to work. Never was stronger and more decisive evidence given against a line'.

In spite of this, and the fact that it was broad gauge, Parliament appears to have been convinced of the arguments in favour of the project, as within three days of the NAH Act, on 3 August 1846 the VNR was authorised with a capital of £550,000 in £20 shares. No doubt the outcome of the application was influenced by the backing of the Jersey family and the close ties with the SWR. An important local event occurred two days later when the standard gauge TVR was officially welcomed to Aberdare. No more was heard of either the WMR or the GE&W.

The first months were devoted to negotiations with the SWR and the local landowners over whose land the railway was intended to pass. One of the most difficult was a Mr William Llewellyn of Dulais Vach Farm, Aberdylais (*sic*), near Neath, over two of whose fields a right of way was sought. He wanted the railway to be unseen, and therefore required a tunnel to be built of stone and brick at ground level, with fenced ends, and decorative parapet. How the matter was resolved is unclear, but a simple though sizeable cutting survives to this day.

At the first board meeting on 11 August 1846, Viscount Villiers was elected Chairman, and Fred Saunders was appointed Secretary at a salary of £300 p.a. Villiers was the eldest son of the Earl of Jersey whom he was to succeed on 3 October 1859, only to die 21 days later. Jersey

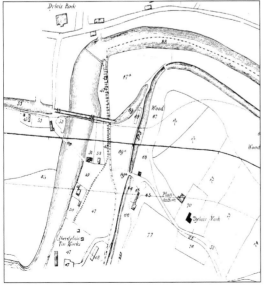

An extract from the submission to Parliament in 1846 showing the location and description of Llewellyn's farm.
House of Lords Record Office.

Aberdylais (sic) Halt, looking north towards Llewellyn's cutting. July 1956.

R. M. Casserley.

Coal trains still use the cutting made through Llewellyn's pasture. 1994.

DD.

was a powerful figure and land-owner in south Wales and had chaired the inaugural meetings of the VNR. Villiers, born in Berkeley Square in 1808, married the elder daughter of the Prime Minister, Sir Robert Peel, and was M.P. for Cirencester from 1844 to 1852. Not surprisingly he was a Conservative and a Free-Trader. He seems to have been a diligent chairman and to

have picked some good people; he was not alone in being unable to control Brunel and it is possible that his father's interests weakened his position in dealing with the docks at Briton Ferry and Swansea. His wife, on the other hand, was no doubt a source of strength, especially in the early days.

A distant view of Neath showing two VNR trains and the short-lived spur leading westward to the South Wales Railway. (see plan page 30).

ILN.

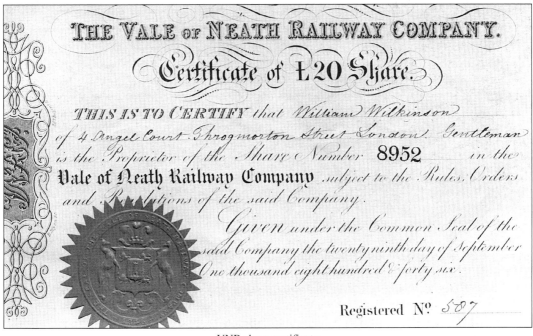

VNR share certificate.

WIMM.

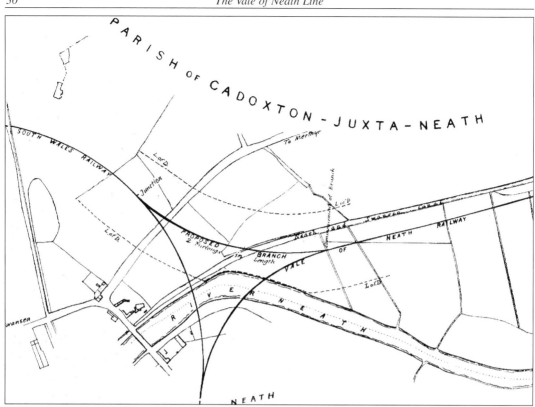

Plan submitted to Parliament in 1847 to construct the westward-facing spur to the SWR at Neath, illustrated on page 29.

House of Lords Record Office.

By the end of September 1846 it had become apparent that there would be difficulty in disposing of all the shares as some 5000 were still unsold. At the end of the following February, the SWR agreed to take up the unwanted shares, and a year later this was confirmed by Act of Parliament; the SWR got the right to appoint up to four directors but a maximum of one third; they were to be barred from voting on SWR matters related to sale or amalgamation. The four directors who were due to retire at the August 1848 shareholder general meeting, including the chairman of the VNR board, were all appointed by the SWR as their directors. In 1856 the SWR was to sell shares causing their entitlement to appoint directors to be reduced to three.

In spite of the depressed state of the economy and the money market, Brunel was told to proceed with the construction and 1847 saw progress. A second bill was submitted to Parliament to permit an additional junction with

the SWR at Neath, facing towards the west, and to agree the running powers from Neath to the Port of Neath and Briton Ferry. The Act, called the VNR Amendment Act 1847, included the surprising provision for a railway to link Aberdare to the mouth of the projected Merthyr tunnel by a line of track climbing up the side of the mountain, with 546 yds at 1 in 16 and 730 yds at 1 in 13. The great Brunel put his signature to this remarkable project. It comes as no surprise to learn that in 1852 permission was obtained not to proceed.

By July, the first construction contract covering 9 miles from Neath had been let. However, because of the general financial situation, the contract for the Merthyr tunnel was postponed until February 1848, when the contract for the shafts and headings was let; the main contract to Hunt, Humphries & Edwards followed in September. Parliament had set up the Railway Commissioners with powers, among other things, to grant extensions of time for the completion of authorised railways. In February 1848 the VNR sought the maximum permitted of two years. Nevertheless by August of that year the whole of the line to the head of the Neath valley was under construction.

The state of the market led to three half-yearly general meetings of shareholders failing to obtain a quorum, once in 1848 and twice in 1849 and caused a number of defaults on the April 1847 call to shareholders which the company had been reluctant to press. In early 1849, £11,696 was in arrears. However one year later arrears started to decrease as the calls rose to cover the construction progress. There was a lesson here for the NAH if only they had been aware. The aim was to open the lower part of the line simultaneously with the opening of the SWR. In the event this was not done as it was felt to be preferable to be able to open all the way to Aberdare.

2-8-0T No. 5241 approaches Aberdulais with a train of empty waggons. May 1964.
John Davies.

0-6-2T No. 6621 crosses the Neath River on the later iron bridge and approaches the South Wales main-line. June 1964.

John Davies.

Former GW 0-6-2T No. 6686 heads an evening service across the river at Neath. June 1964.

John Davies.

2-8-2T No. 7214 is about to pass under the South Wales main-line *en route* to the docks at Swansea. January 1964.

John Davies.

The works on the Merthyr tunnel now gave cause for concern. Two contractors failed after finding obstructions they had not provided for at the depth of 650 ft. In the summer of 1850, the contract for the line from Hirwaun to Aberdare was let, after recognition at the end of 1849 that Aberdare would now be the first objective, Merthyr inevitably second. Judging by the way the business of the company eventually developed, with emphasis on coal movement down the Vale of Neath from Aberdare and a fairly small reliance on passenger traffic, this may not have been the disadvantage it at first appeared. Indeed, although there is no evidence of this, it is possible that the directors had realised that Merthyr's pre-eminence as an iron producing centre was diminishing as its local supply of iron-ore ran out.

The original VNR Act of 3 August 1846 had indicated that the terminus in Aberdare should be at or near the TVR station. In accordance with powers obtained by the Gadlys colliery, the VNR was anxious to cross the Taff Vale on the level to gain access to the Gadlys mine and was thinking of approaching the Aberdare Railway, a TVR subsidiary, which owned the Taff Vale Aberdare branch. They eventually decided not to press the point while raising the possibility of an interchange arrangement at the TVR station and joint use of the Taff Vale facility. The TVR response was unhelpful so the Vale of Neath built its own station at Aberdare on the opposite side of the river. Funding of the Aberdare extension was by a further call in July and the issue of the first debentures authorised by an Extraordinary General Meeting held at the Castle Hotel Neath, in November 1850; the original Act permitted this additional method of financing once the whole of the initial share capital was subscribed and 50% paid up.

An engraving, ca. 1855, showing the covered station and engine shed at Aberdare, and, in the distance, the newly constructed Dare Viaduct.

WIMM.

At a board meeting on 15 March 1850, H.A. Bruce, the M.P. for Merthyr, and one day to be chairman, gave notice that he was going to recommend at the next board meeting that Brunel's salary be reduced from £1000 p.a. to £600 in view of the unreasonable time it was taking to complete the line. This was deferred until the next meeting, due to take place in London, and was not pursued. The works were not however proceeding without problems. Apart from the difficulties with the Merthyr tunnel, the extensive earthworks and retaining walls, the Gwrelych (*sic*) viaduct, and the crossing of the Neath river at Neath were all giving trouble. After Mr Bruce's outburst, matters deteriorated further, because the winter of 1850/1851 was unusually wet. This caused a landslip half a mile below the Pencaedrain tunnel near the head of the Glyn Neath Bank. 80 yards of an embankment across a gully slipped 45 yards down the hill; Brunel decided to replace it with a timber viaduct. Nevertheless work on the timber bridge over the river Neath at Neath and the embankment over the marshes was nearly complete by February 1851. Furthermore the track was being doubled from Neath as far as Gelli Tarw Junction some 1⅓ miles east of Hirwaun station; this was the point where the Merthyr line would leave what now became the main line. Brunel still expected to be able to open to Aberdare in June, yet it was as late as February before the orders were placed for the first rolling stock.

Six locomotives were ordered from Robert Stephenson and tenders were called for the following stock:

- 6 closed 3rd class carriages
- 6 open ditto
- 6 2nd class carriages
- 6 composite 1st and 2nd class carriages
- 1 open excursion carriage
- 12 general merchandise trucks
- 50 (increased later to 120) flat coal trucks
- 10 coal waggons

The flat coal trucks enabled the coal to be loaded in bottom-opening boxes which caused less breakage of coal when the boxes were lowered into the hold of a ship. This very early form of containerisation had its limitations, however, and was to prove expensive.

Preparations for operations were also being made in other areas. In May 1851, Joshua Williams was appointed General Superintendent; it was decided to adopt GWR traffic management procedures, and the uniforms were modelled on those of the GWR. Thirty days notice of opening was given to the Railway Commissioners in May, but when June came, it was impossible to open as the retaining wall below a cliff opposite the Abernant Works, at Glyn Neath, had collapsed in heavy rain. This was, perhaps, just as well, as there was no rolling stock; nor could the GWR help, in spite of Brunel. The shareholders must have been disheartened as they failed to form a quorum at the general meeting called in Cardiff for 30 August, when Brunel reported that one locomotive was on the road to Chepstow, another was coming shortly and several carriages would be delivered 'in a few days'. However the following stations were under construction and were expected to be ready for opening, now due in September :

> Neath (joint with the SWR)
> Aberdulais
> Resolven
> Glyn Neath
> Hirwaun
> Merthyr Rd—a temporary facility, pending
>   completion of the line to Merthyr
> Aberdare

Eventually, on 23 September 1851, a ceremonial train carried the directors and friends from Neath to Aberdare. It was hauled by a GWR locomotive, which appears to have had some difficulty with the Glyn Neath Bank. One of the speakers assured the gathering that once the new VNR engine arrived it would be able to move much heavier trains without difficulty. (It is unclear what had happened to this new VNR locomotive, a 4-4-0 saddle tank, reported by Brunel only a month previously to be *en route* to Chepstow.) However the party eventually reached Aberdare where lunch was served; on the return, a band provided by Crawshays Works

The VNR third class iron carriage.

WIMM: GW Coll.

Model of VNR passenger train, depicting locomotive No. 10, with a covered first class carriage, an open third class vehicle, and a horse-box. The VNR made a virtue of the primitive third class accommodation by advertising: 'To all excursionists and tourists; the directors of the Vale of Neath Railway Co. have provided first class and open excursion carriages especially adapted for viewing the justly celebrated scenery of this valley and its inhabitants.'

WIMM.

This model of a VNR coal train shows the coal boxes (4 per truck) and conventional coal waggons.

WIMM.

Resolven Station staff on the down platform.

R. W. Kidner Coll.

General view of Hirwaun Station looking east in April 1964. A short mineral branch from the Penderyn Quarry entered behind the West Box on the left.

R. H. Marrows.

was picked up at Hirwaun and they provided music for the ride back down to Neath, where a public breakfast was presided over by the Mayor.

Business began the next day, with three trains each way on weekdays and two on Sundays, using hired locomotives. Because the line was double track from Neath as far as Hirwaun, it was possible to operate with two separate trains, the last into Aberdare spending the night under cover of the station roof. Journey time from Neath to Aberdare was 70 minutes.

In February 1851 the contract for the completion of the Merthyr tunnel had been let to

Ritson, who had successfully constructed the Pencaedrain tunnel. At the same time a single track line from Gelli Tarw Junction was being laid towards the tunnel south entrance as far as a colliery at Werfa. By February 1853 the tunnel was nearly complete, but the branch was not finally opened until 2 November that year. The new station at Merthyr, described by Brunel as 'comprehensive and substantial', was located close to the High Street, and was to become eventually the only station in the town. Thus a typical Brunel train shed appeared in the middle of Merthyr.

Song of the Town Clerk:

"The railway to Merthyr cried Coke quite enchanted
We'll make up our valley - the thought is divine.
The project conceived, he then only wanted
A lot of shareholders to take up the line.
He flew to Lord Jersey and laid it before him;
His lordship, delighted, cried "Do it we will".
He went to Brunel who declared he could bore him
An easy way through the most difficult hill.

The public exclaimed "We could ne'er be investing
Our cash in a scheme more inviting and fair.
Your road is the bank for our fortunes to rest in
And pay 10% per original share !"
So the bargain was struck and the money paid in -
Judiciously spent upon tunnel and tip -
And now the directors with blessings are laden,
Instead of with valueless forfeited scrip!"

The final verse of the song ran as follows:

"Sweet valley of Neath, may thy beauty prevail
On the fares who are fairest to rush to our rail !
May thy coal and thy iron our traffic augment
And our shares pay us (something unheard of) per cent."

Song of the Town Clerk: September 1851.
Monmouthshire Merlin.

Merthyr Tunnel west portal in a view which illustrates the generous dimensions of the bore. The later retaining walls provide evidence of the instability of the terrain.

Cynon Valley Borough Libraries.

Merthyr Tunnel east portal on the last day of service, 29 December 1962; locomotive No. 6416. Whereas the western portal was built to accommodate double track, the eastern portal, as may be seen, was single track only.

W. Spurrier.

As a result of opening the line through to Merthyr High Street, the temporary arrangements at Merthyr Road became redundant. Merthyr had been seen as an important source of passenger traffic and it had therefore seemed worthwhile to provide a temporary station, even on a bleak wind- and rain-swept moor some 5 miles from the town and

the other side of a mountain of some 1,800 ft in height. 37,000 people used the VNR between its opening on 24 September and the end of December, and the management expressed satisfaction that, contrary to expectations, the railway was able to trade at a profit in the first three months of operation. Once the Merthyr branch was open, Merthyr Road station building was abandoned and converted into two dwellings.

It was not until six months after the railway opened to Aberdare in April 1852 that the first coal trains started running. Until then, Briton Ferry was not ready to handle either coal trains or iron ore imports, and traffic through Swansea had been delayed by the need for extra dredging. Nevertheless, in anticipation, the VNR had been looking at the pricing of coal movements as a result of enquiries from the collieries around Aberdare and reckoned on being able to compete with the TVR on the basis of charging one penny per ton per mile for 28 miles, on the assumption that the port charges at Swansea were no more than at Cardiff. They were helped by the greater capacity of broad gauge trucks—10 tons costing 2¼ pence per ton compared with 4½—5 tons costing 3 pence on the narrow gauge. The interest of the collieries was such that in early

Merthyr Road station site looking east, 1995.

GBJ.

0-6-0PT No. 6433 leaves Hirwaun on a sunny frosty morning in November 1963 bound for Llwydcoed, Abernant and Merthyr.

John Davies.

Rhydycar Junction, looking west, towards Merthyr Tunnel, 1964. The Brecon line curves away to the right.
W. Spurrier.

Mardy Junction, showing the TVR bearing left. The VNR crossed both the TVR's original line to Merthyr (Plymouth Street) and the River Taff by the substantial girder bridge. August 1967.
R. H. Marrows.

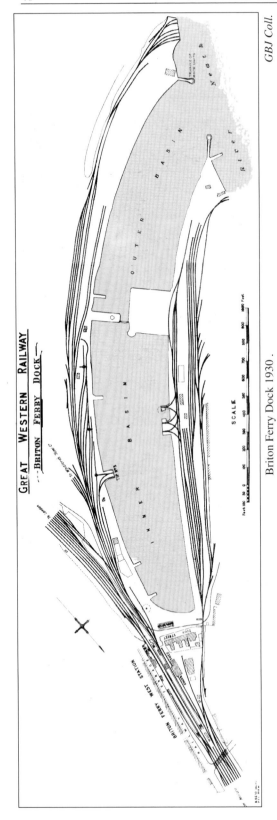

GBJ Coll.

Briton Ferry Dock 1930.

1852, lines were surveyed into the Dare and Aman valleys, west and south of Aberdare, and a decision was taken to extend the main line by ½ mile to the head of the Aberdare canal. Seven pits had been in operation in the Aberdare valley in 1845; now there were 16 with another 12 being opened. These developments were authorised by the VNR Act 1852.

The extension to the head of the canal was to simplify handling. It was the practice of the collieries to load coal into the boxes previously described. These were either loaded direct into canal barges or carried to the canal by tramway. To reach the VNR they then had to be conveyed to the canal head and transferred again into tram-trucks for carriage to the VNR yard. Here they were lifted onto VNR platform coal waggons by hand-operated standing cranes.

By the end of 1852 the mood was optimistic; expenditure as a percentage of receipts had fallen from 66% to 46.8%, even after the inclusion of permanent way maintenance from the time of hand-over from the contractors. A 1½% dividend was declared. 93,437 passengers were carried in the half year, but it was already noticeable that replacing brake blocks on carriages and goods waggons as a result of the severe gradients was a significant expense. Three more locomotives were ordered, together with two more 3rd class carriages and two 4-wheeled vans for general goods and luggage, particularly for the use of passengers using the trains on market days. Evidence of a substantial trade in crockery at this time is revealed by the requirement for suitable shelving in these vans. In view of the class of person using the line, two 2nd class carriages were to be disposed of.

The first of many accidents on the railway occurred soon after operations began. Near Glyn Neath, a train ran past the signalman, after being unable to stop in a distance of ½ a mile, and ran into two waggons awaiting unloading on the main line. In July, an engine ran into a siding and damaged a GWR waggon because the pointsman had forgotten to move back the points. This led to new rules: in future all points were to be kept locked, and riding on the footplate was to be permitted only with written consent. It was also decided to dispense with the height restriction on

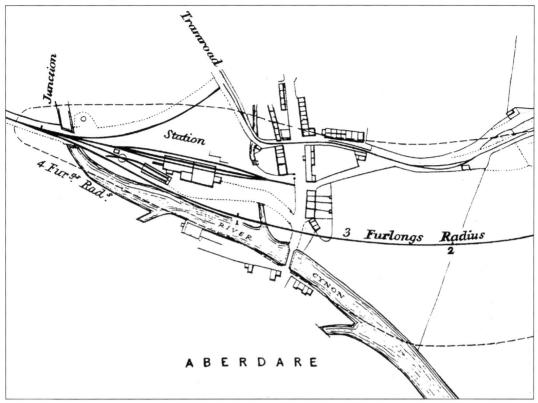

Plan of Aberdare station prepared to support the 1852 application to Parliament to extend the line to the Canal Head.

House of Lords Record Office.

personnel, as it was felt that intelligent and able servants were being excluded thereby from working on the railway. As might be expected, other accidents were particularly associated with the gradients. For instance in 1854, a truck ran away from Hirwaun station, down the line to Gelli Tarw where the pointsman had the presence of mind to switch it towards Merthyr instead of letting it continue down the 1 in 50 slope to Aberdare; it came to a stop at Llwydcoed station, a run of some 4 miles in all. In the same year, two more waggons rolled down the slope from Hirwaun station towards the junction; this time the alert switchman diverted them down the Dare branch where they came to rest. Very occasionally goods or mineral trains did the same thing and this practice continued to be an option for the signalman at Gelli Tarw until the introduction of fitted waggons. Even more dramatic must have been the case of the six-wheeled truck being taken from Merthyr to the other side of the tunnel to pick up some rails; it was hauled by two horses, which at the tunnel entrance were detached to enable the draught chains to be shortened; in the process the truck began to roll back to Merthyr, and did not stop until it got there.

Average receipts per week per mile had risen from £10 16s. 0d. in the first half of 1852 to £34 0s. 0d. in the second half of 1853. The dividend was raised to 2%. By the end of 1853, with the benefit of the Merthyr branch now in operation, 148,579 passengers were carried in the half year, an increase of 122% in the period since opening to Merthyr. However delay was still being experienced with the Dare and Aman branches, and in the delivery of new rolling stock. Brunel reported to the shareholders in slightly defensive vein that despite the weather, curves and gradients, and the weight of the coal traffic, the railway was working well.

Ca. 1930 O.S. map of Gelli Tarw with inset view looking east, towards Merthyr. June 1963.

Due to delays of about a year in taking delivery of new locomotives, the costs of maintenance rose. Thus at the end of the first half of 1854, costs as a proportion of receipts, a key yardstick of performance, were also up from 46.39% to 48.45%. However, by the end of that year, the delivery of three more powerful locomotives for the Glyn and Aberdare banks brought expenses down to 41.2%. An outbreak of cholera at Merthyr restricted travel to local journeys, but the dividend was raised to 3½%,

share capital was increased by £45,000, and an application was made to Parliament to raise an additional £120,000. This was authorised by the VNR (Capital) Act 1855. In the same year Parliament also approved an extension from Aberdare for 1¾ miles to Middle Duffryn, by the Aberdare Valley Railway Act. This company, leased to the VNR and finally purchased in 1865, was to provide the link with the extension of the NAH line from Pontypool, which Parliament was to authorise in 1857.

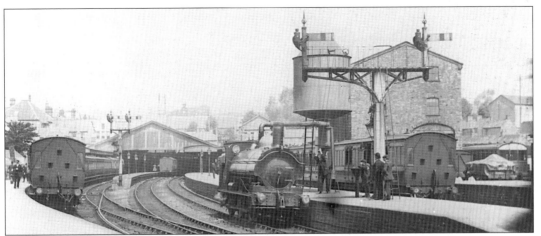

Merthyr High Street Station in Edwardian times, with GW 0-6-0 saddle tank No. 2069 and a Steam Rail Motor (extreme right background).

Courtesy C. C. Green.

0-6-0T No. 6427 heading the Hirwaun auto-train under Brunel's train-shed at Merthyr, with visiting LNER luggage van and *Cordon* gas wagon, extreme right.

WIMM: GW Coll.

Merthyr: interior of Brunel's Station.

WIMM: GW Coll.

The view westward at Llwydcoed Station in BR days.
National Monuments Record for Wales.

Abernant station looking towards Merthyr in May 1961. Both this station and Llwydcoed were built to serve the expansion of the Aberdare suburbs up the north side of the Cynon valley.

NMRW.

The bridge carrying the VNR Merthyr branch over the Glamorganshire Canal near Rhydycar Junction. 1994.

GBJ.

Joint Line Junction looking east, with VNR in the foreground and GW/RR beyond the box. Ca. 1925.

W. Spurrier Coll.

Brunel's Dare Viaduct in 1893.

WIMM: GW Coll.

Very few photographs exist of the summer excursions to Barry or Porthcawl, from the Dare and Aman branches, but at least one such train was recorded crossing the Dare Viaduct.

R.H. Marrows Coll.

VNR 0-6-0T No. 10, 11 or 12 shunting near Bwllfa Colliery, ca. 1870.

Cynon Valley Borough Libraries.

The Dare and Aman branches had been due for completion in August 1854, but shortage of ballast, among other factors, was limiting progress. Brunel delivered a little homily on the importance of good ballast; he was particularly interested in the subject because, for the sake of economy, these two branches were laid with Barlow rail, the 12 or 13 inch wide rail which was laid directly in the ballast thus avoiding the use of sleepers. It was generally not a success. A year later hard facts had to be faced and the real cause of delay acknowledged, resulting in the contractor being sacked. The new contractor, Eassie by name, had much experience which included the building of stations. The Merthyr Dare colliery was reached by November 1854. Eassie then pressed on to the end of the branch at Bwllfa colliery, from where coal was first moved in June 1857. The Aman remained inoperative until sometime after 1857, this delay being due more to a lack of trade than any fault on the part of the contractor. Shareholders debated the wisdom of building a railway if there was no trade, but the management argued that many new pits would only be developed if a railway was first in place.

Progress was positive until the end of 1857, with the coal trade showing dramatic development from 708 tons in 1851 to some 400,000 tons in 1857. Iron ore imports began in early 1857 and passenger numbers stabilised around 400,000 journeys per annum. In the first half of 1857 a record dividend of 4¾ % was achieved; in the second half of the year a coal strike put a stop to coal movements, and although costs were held at 47.4 %, the dividend had to drop back to 4½%. Thereafter, against the background of a severe monetary crisis, the results deteriorated every half year, until the second half of 1860. The iron ore traffic continued to grow, but this was a mixed blessing as it was all uphill work and therefore expensive.

By the end of 1855, problems with the permanent way had led to a decision to start replacing the track with stronger rails, which was carried out selectively but especially on the banks. By 1858, this was becoming a significant cost burden and by October 1859 it was decided that the company could do the job cheaper than

the contractor, Ritson. Joshua Williams had taken over as General Manager responsible for engineering as well as traffic at the end of 1858, and by August 1859 he was characteristically looking for signs of recovery; nevertheless the directors were obliged to forgo the dividend as costs were still rising, especially on track and rolling stock maintenance, and the half year figures at the end of 1859 were little up on 1858. On 24 October 1859 the chairman died, 21 days after inheriting his father's title. It was also the year of Brunel's death. The chairman was succeeded by H.A. Bruce, a barrister and the Liberal M.P. for Merthyr from 1852 to 1868. He eventually became Lord President of the Council, having in 1863 become Secretary of State for the Home Department. In 1873 he became Baron Aberdare of Duffryn, where he had been born in 1815. Admiral Warde was appointed Deputy Chairman. He was a local resident and an able and helpful support to management. By the end of the first half of 1860 the new chairman had again to recommend no dividend to the shareholders as traffic was still in decline.

The 1st Lord Aberdare and his family photographed in about 1890 outside Duffryn House.
Cynon Valley Borough Libraries.

In this depressing situation, it had been decided at the August 1859 General Meeting to appoint a Committee of Investigation, consisting of three directors, one auditor, and three shareholders, to examine the future of the company. The SWR asked to be represented also, but it was decided that, although they could witness the discussions, they should not be allowed to vote. Bruce was its chairman. On 1 October T.E. Harrison, chief engineer of the North Eastern Railway, was appointed to investigate the track, the rolling stock, and the traffic arrangements, to advise on alterations to the methods of working, and as to the relative advantages of Swansea and Briton Ferry as ports. He reported on 24 November, and his report, summarised here, was adopted :

1. The last three locomotives which had been ordered for working on the banks were too heavy and each axle bore too great a weight for the track; they should be converted to tender engines. Compensating levers were to be fitted to enable the adjustment of the weight carried on each axle.

2. He recommended a careful review of the type of waggon used for the carriage of coal. In order to minimise breakage of the coal on loading, it was general VNR practice to use the flat waggons, which each carried four containers or boxes. The drawbacks were the higher first cost, and the extra weight of these vehicles over a normal waggon, (some 50% more), which increased the cost of hauling them. Harrison observed that since the advantage in breakage virtually ceased once the hold was half-filled, the appeal of this type of waggon to the colliery owners should be carefully tested.

3. Briton Ferry was considered the best port for the VNR, but access to Swansea would also be desirable in view of its importance, though not while the current split management arrangements with the SWR persisted; these were likely to cause any increase in trade to lead to congestion. Independent access to Swansea across the flat land by the sea would be most attractive.

4. The broad gauge was expensive to build and maintain but no change other than using heavy rails on cross rather than longitudinal sleepers was feasible, until the SWR introduced mixed gauge. The report was in no doubt however that conversion to standard gauge was desirable for the VNR in the longer term.

5. The company should carry out its own maintenance of locomotives and track.

Glyn Neath station buildings (up side) showing signs of a need for the re-building which was shortly to follow. 1952.

WIMM: GW Coll.

An early engraving of Glyn Neath Station, indicating generous covered accommodation.

Neath Antiquarian Society.

Glyn Neath Station, looking up the bank. Ca 1910.

Great Western Trust, Didcot.

Looking up the Glyn Neath bank at Pontwalby Halt; the space once occupied by broad-gauge track is clearly visible. July 1956.

R. M. Casserley.

British Rhondda Signal Box. The perspective of the box demonstrates the severity of the Glyn Neath bank at this point. This box had the reputation among footplate-men that if the name was illegible from a descending train, the locomotive was out of control. June 1963.

R. H. Marrows.

Pontwalby Viaduct, looking down the Vale of Neath. British Rhondda Signal Box and sidings are also visible. No date.

GBJ Coll.

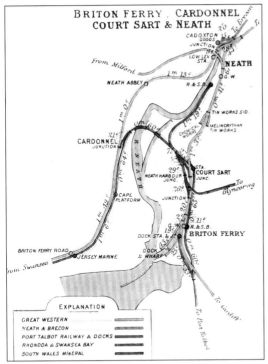

Railways around Neath: 1913.

Railway Clearing House.

The inadequacy of the two ports of Neath and Swansea had been a thorn in the flesh of the VNR since the beginning. Indeed, it was the absence of a suitable rail link to the wharf at Briton Ferry that had delayed the start of coal traffic for six months after the opening for passenger traffic, on 24 September 1851. The wharf was in any case inadequate to cope with the growth in coal exports and iron ore imports stimulated by the VNR. Access to Swansea was by courtesy of the SWR and involved scaling a serious incline at Skewen of 1 in 90, which required the trains to be split. Additionally the locomotives loaned to the SWR by the GWR for the purpose were not the best to be found. In order to improve the situation, the VNR had over time adopted two strategies: the first with regard to Briton Ferry was to improve the docks; this had been in hand since 1853 with Ritson as contractor. The VNR subscribed £20,000 towards the cost, but, by 1859, the work had come to a standstill, due to a lack of funds. In 1860 the VNR got Parliamentary approval to guarantee the interest on the unissued share capital of the

Briton Ferry Co. to the extent of £40,000, which enabled the work to proceed and to be completed in 1861.

The second strategy concerned Swansea. VNR policy there had been to rely on the SWR. After all they were the largest single shareholder and the chairman was a director of the SWR, and, unlike the position at Briton Ferry, steps had been taken over time by the harbour authorities to upgrade the facilities in the port. A problem arose in 1859 however when matters came to a head over rail access. It was to be partially alleviated in April 1861 when the SWR finally agreed to the VNR operating its own coal trains to Swansea over the SWR main line, and by the reopening of the upgraded North Dock in November 1860, but what was really needed was an additional and preferably standard gauge railway to improve the access to Swansea.

At this point the NAH came into the picture. Although its original ambitions extended no further than Merthyr, matters had changed by 1854 when the NAH, with LNWR backing, had sought unsuccessfully to get Parliamentary approval to extend their line from Quakers Yard as far as Swansea. When in 1857 Parliament approved the extension of the NAH as far as Aberdare, the NAH suggested to the VNR taking extra land from Middle Duffryn to Navigation colliery to enable the VNR to extend to this colliery, in return for which the VNR was to take extra land beside their track to enable the NAH to extend to Aberdare. This the VNR turned down. Then in June 1860, just when the NAH was in the process of being absorbed into the West Midland Railway (West MR), a meeting was held to discuss joint use of the VNR station at Aberdare. The meeting also considered the options for creating an interchange, extending the VNR as far as the Navigation colliery, and extending the NAH standard gauge over portions of the VNR. By November this had grown into a proposal from the now West MR to link end-on with the VNR at Middle Duffryn; they offered the VNR 5% less operating expenses on the cost of laying an additional narrow gauge rail throughout and an extension from Neath to Swansea. In addition, they proposed not to support any other schemes to make a new link

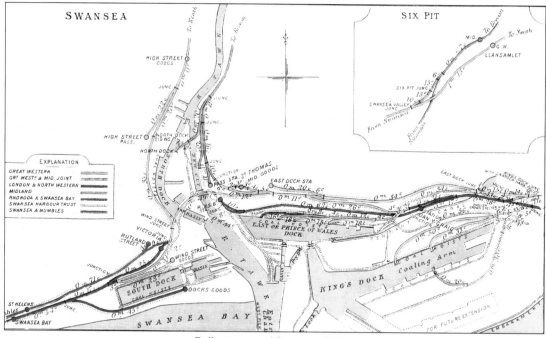

Railways around Swansea: 1913.

Railway Clearing House.

between Neath and Swansea. Predictably, the SWR directors on the VNR board objected to this proposal and tried to discourage the chairman from pursuing the matter, arguing that the West MR offer was 'too crude and undefined'. At this time the VNR were nervous that if they did not get reasonable terms from the SWR to operate their own and West MR trains to Swansea, the West MR would build their own line to the Swansea Vale and gain independent access. Accordingly, by a majority, the board took steps to implement two of Harrison's recommendations— first to convert to mixed gauge, though disagreements between the directors caused the opportunity to have the West MR finance the third rail to be missed; second, they allowed the VNR name to be associated with a separate project to build a new line from Swansea to Neath.

This scheme, resulting in the eventual formation of the Swansea & Neath Railway (SNR), was promoted by a London firm of solicitors with the backing of the SWR, concerned to preserve the broad gauge domination of Swansea. In addition to an extension of the VNR, the scheme included a

Joshua Williams.

DD Coll.

direct link across the Neath river to Briton Ferry and another local railway, the South Wales Mineral. This part of the scheme was rejected in Parliament following protest from the VNR and the Neath Harbour Commissioners. Thereupon, the SWR withdrew their backing. When the bill appeared before the House of Lords, the VNR had stepped in as promoter, and the Swansea and Neath Railway Act received Royal Assent on 6 August 1861; it was to be a broad gauge line, but with the proviso that if the VNR became mixed gauge, the SNR was to do likewise. This was an unusual railway in that it was laid with mixed gauge from the outset and with transverse sleepers, chairs and double-headed rail. The SNR opened in July 1863. Passenger services started on 1 August from a new station at Neath to a temporary platform on a site rented from the Town for 1s. per annum at Swansea, Wind Street. There were intermediate stations at Neath Abbey and Briton Ferry Road. By this time the SWR was finally buried in the GWR by full amalgamation and, by the VNR Act 1863, the SNR was to be amalgamated with the VNR.

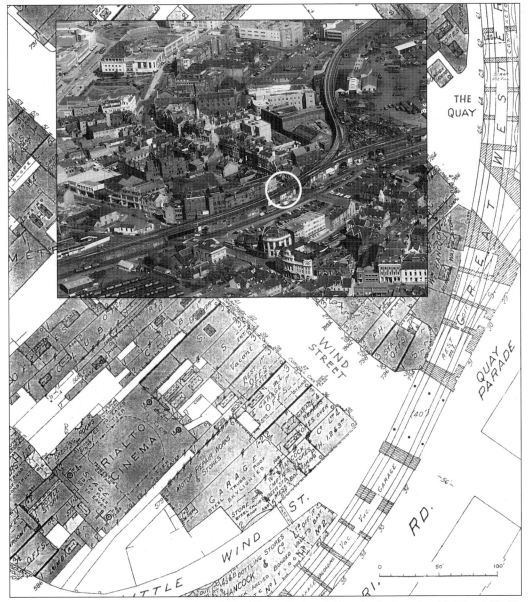

A 1930s plan showing the probable location of Wind Street Station, believed to be in arches No.32 and 33. (See page 101).

Swansea City Archives and WIMM.

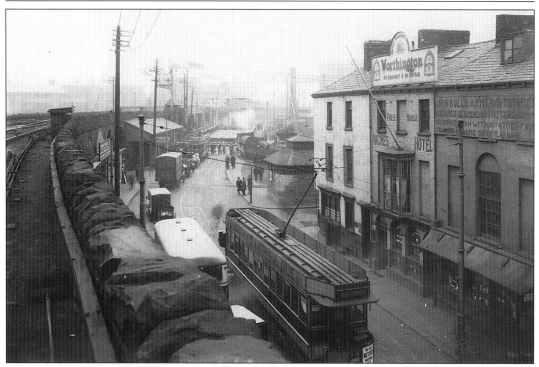

A 1928 view, looking east, from the vicinity of Swansea Wind Street Station, showing the elevated aspect of the Vale of Neath line and, at street level, the fascinating queue of traffic awaiting the closing of the North Dock drawbridge (middle distance).

WIMM: GW Coll.

Briton Ferry Road Station, SNR. No date.

WIMM: GW Coll.

Neath Abbey Station. No date.

R. H. Marrows Coll.

Neath Abbey Station; SNR opening, July 1863.

ILN.

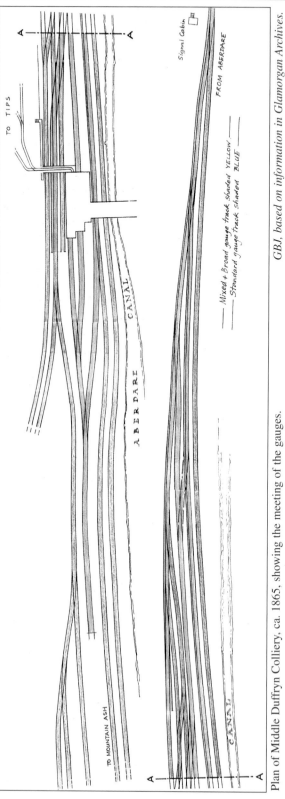

Plan of Middle Duffryn Colliery, ca. 1865, showing the meeting of the gauges.

GBJ, based on information in Glamorgan Archives.

Another provision of the SNR Act covered the links between the VNR and the TVR west of Aberdare, at the Gadlys colliery. In 1853 the colliery had built a broad gauge line to the VNR across the TVR branch and it was intended that interchange between the TVR and the Vale of Neath should now be made near this point in order to coincide with the completion of mixed gauge on the VNR. The VNR completed their side of the bargain but the TVR, seeing less to be gained and much to be lost, dragged their feet. In May 1861, a bad accident occurred at this crossing when engine number 11 of the VNR hit engine number 11 of the Gadlys colliery, killing the driver and fireman. A verdict of accidental death was recorded.

The major outstanding issue in the VNR board room was still the question of the link at Middle Duffryn; after the difference of opinion between the directors over the West MR proposition, discussion continued at management level and heads of agreement were eventually reached and endorsed by a majority of the board. The VNR were particularly concerned that the weight of West MR locomotives would not be greater than those of the VNR; clearly Harrison had made his mark. However, it seems as though the West MR were still considering the alternative of linking to the Taff Vale at Mountain Ash, short of Middle Duffryn, and thereby reducing capital investment. Indeed in 1861 the West MR sought powers to withdraw altogether from the proposal to link with the VNR, relying solely on that to the TVR, but depriving themselves thereby of the through route beyond Aberdare. This may have reflected an awakening to commercial realism, or it may have been intended as a tactical threat to the VNR; if so it succeeded, for early in 1862 the VNR decided independently to lay a third rail throughout their system at their own expense, and got Parliamentary approval to do so in July of the same year. The work started early in 1863 and the board had thus taken steps to fulfil the two Harrison recommendations with regard to access to

Swansea and narrowing the gauge, and were doing all that was needed on their side to make a standard gauge link between Middle Duffryn and Swansea. Indeed it looks as though the NAH and their successors had decided to let the Vale of Neath make the running.

The Great Western now realised that a standard gauge line to Swansea was likely to materialise, and was concerned that the West MR through its constituents, especially the Oxford, Worcester and Wolverhampton Railway, had a close relationship with the London and North Western Railway; the Great Western therefore set about ensuring that the West MR fell into its own net; accordingly after intense negotiation, the West MR was amalgamated with the GWR in August 1863, shortly after full absorption of the South Wales. As part of the deals made to avoid opposition in Parliament, the GWR agreed with the VNR to complete the line from Pontypool to Middle Duffryn and to make an end-on link there so that through trains could operate from Hereford to Swansea. In return the VNR was to complete its third rail as quickly as possible.

The Vale of Neath had told the West Midland in May 1863 that the line would be ready to receive narrow gauge trains at Middle Duffryn by June, but found it necessary to remind them of the advantage of such a link compared with running onto the Taff Vale at Mountain Ash. It therefore looks as though the final decision by the then amalgamating managements, to opt for the VNR link as well as the TVR, was not taken until July 1863. This may have been further prompted by the passing of the bill authorising the Brecon and Merthyr and LNWR to enter Merthyr over the VNR, which would give the Vale of Neath another narrow gauge link to the Midlands and the north. Then on 1 August the VNR wrote to the Great Western pressing for action and seeking a meeting to discuss through traffic arrangements between Hereford and Swansea. The GWR reply said that instructions to complete with 'all possible expedition' had been given. On 3 October there was still no progress from the GWR and Joshua Williams was authorised to meet them to try to make arrangements and to negotiate with Powell's Colliery about a temporary junction. Meanwhile

the LNWR, who had running powers over the former NAH, approached the Vale of Neath for the same, and were well received. On 28 December 1863 the VNR celebrated the completion of mixing the gauge by running a standard gauge locomotive and brake van, borrowed from the Swansea Vale Railway, all the way from Swansea docks to Middle Duffryn; Joshua Williams rode in the van. The first standard gauge train over the VNR was a coal train from Gadlys colliery, hauled by a locomotive borrowed from the LNWR. Two of these were retained by the VNR until their own standard gauge locomotives were ready in 1864.

It now transpired that the owner of the vital land needed by the Great Western to make the link at Middle Duffryn was asking £1000. The GWR considered this too much, and therefore proposed to go to Parliament for a compulsory purchase, which would postpone progress indefinitely. By this time, Joshua Williams' frustration must have been intense. He went up to Paddington and returned to Wales with authority to negotiate the land purchase. By 14 November he was telegraphing the Chairman of the GWR to tell him that he had got possession for £800. Eventually a temporary connection was made on 19 March 1864, but only because Joshua Williams, at the request of Nixons who had a ship loading at Swansea, had persuaded the GWR to get together a large workforce and build a temporary junction; thus it was only under strong pressure from the Vale of Neath that the link was finally made. No doubt Joshua Williams' wrath was extreme when he realised the ship had sailed on 17 March. Official opening for goods traffic was delayed until April 1864, whereupon two trains per day were operated; they carried little freight and the only company which appeared to be keen to exploit the new link was the LNWR. After further complaint, the GWR directors now in place of the SWR on the Vale of Neath board protested that it was the company's officers, not the directors, who were frustrating progress. After personal intervention again at chairman level, the line was finally opened to passenger trains on 5 October. The through line then operated for 100 years. The rest of the VNR system was mixed

General view of Middle Duffryn in 1969. The colliery was located beyond the Aberaman Phurnacite Plant, since demolished.

WIMM: NCB Coll.

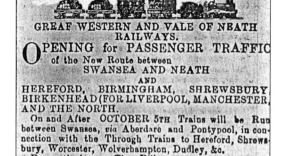

Advertisement, placed in the *Monmouthshire Merlin* on 3 October 1864 by the GWR and VNR, announcing the new route from Swansea to Birkenhead, made possible by completing the link at Middle Duffryn.

gauge by the end of the year, except for the station at Merthyr, which became mixed in 1867. By that time the VNR was no more, as it was absorbed retroactively into the GWR on 1 February 1865 by an act passed in 1866.

The Vale of Neath chairman had been approached by Richard Potter, the Great Western chairman, initially with an offer to lease the VNR. This developed into talks about a take-over and the question of the future dividend for VNR shareholders became the most critical issue. The VNR tried to hold out for 5½%. On 18 October 1864, Joshua Williams wrote at length to Potter; besides describing the merits of the recently completed link at Middle Duffryn, he could not refrain from casting comment on the GWR's attitude to the coal business compared with that shown by the Midland and the Great Northern.

He then went on to argue the value to the GWR of the VNR. It had just declared a dividend of 4½% and would only need £1,700 per half year of extra contribution to achieve 5%; acquisition would save the GWR the cost of mixing gauge on the South Wales main line to Newport, and the contract the GWR had made to buy steam coal for locomotives from Aberdare would be more economically supplied over the Vale of Neath if it were in GWR ownership. He also reminded the GWR of the increased competition to the north from the LNWR, the Cambrian and the Neath & Brecon. In the end the GWR held out for 5.0625% with a minimum of £85,000 and this was accepted. Bruce wrote to Nash Edwards Vaughan, who had succeeded him as chairman at the beginning of 1863, advising acceptance of the GWR terms. He argued that since the VNR would soon need additional capital, it would be a long time before more than 5½% could be earned on the total capital; the line would always be expensive to work and maintain, and there were signs of increasing competition from new lines, while the VNR could in any case never be compared to the Taff Vale.

Meanwhile from 1861 the fortunes of the VNR had been improving. Coal movements revived as a result of taking over the haulage of their own trains into Swansea, and already in the second half of 1860 were up from 219,517 to 257,221 tons, enabling a dividend of 2½% to be restored. In the first half of 1861, coal shipments leapt to 330,035 tons, and the dividend was raised to 3½%, in spite of a heavy cost burden associated with relaying the track, and the greater operating expenses associated with running their own locomotives over the SWR. In the second half of the year coal movements rose 43% which represented a real increase in market share, achieved partly because Briton Ferry was now attracting a better class of shipping to its new wharf opened earlier in the year. The dividend was held at 3%. In 1862 the rate of improvement slowed and the dividend was raised to 3½ %, though in the second half coal movements again rose strongly by a further 25%.

By the end of the first half of 1863, the dividend was held at 3¼ % ; at the end of the year it was back to 4%.

From the outset the VNR had suffered a fatal flaw. The decision at that first meeting in London to operate in alliance with the South Wales and the GW had handicapped the railway with what emerged as the wrong gauge, operationally and commercially, though it is questionable whether the capital cost of the line was excessive at just over £21,000 per mile. That early decision had also caused the board to be incapable of acting strongly to secure their vital interest. They repeatedly spoke of their inability to do anything about the dock facilities and access; it was out of their hands. Earlier attention to the Briton Ferry Dock and access to Swansea could have protected earnings in the late 50s, but the burden of having the great Brunel as engineer lay at the heart of their problems. Not only were his ideas questionable, as with the gauge chosen for a mineral line and the weight of the locomotives, but he seemed to have too much on his plate to give as much attention to either the construction or the operations as the difficulty of the terrain required.

What really saved the VNR and enabled it to perform better than the standard gauge NAH was the quality of management from Chairman down. In this respect the VNR was undoubtedly fortunate in Joshua Williams. He seems to have had a hard time over the Harrison report and in June 1860 tendered his resignation, having been offered a job at the Aberdylais (*sic*) works. However the board voted against allowing him to accept it. They deprecated any interference in their right to appoint or remove executive officers and, accordingly, Joshua Williams dutifully continued to work for the VNR. It does not seem to have affected his enthusiasm and by 1864 he was receiving a salary increase to £1000 a year in consideration of his valuable services and talents. The GWR eventually rewarded him by appointing him Superintendent for South Wales.

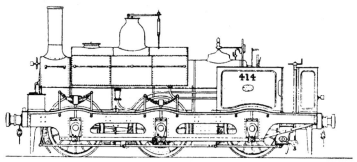

Vale of Neath Railway 0-6-0T No. 21
As G.W.R. No. 414
Built by R. Stephenson & Co., 1864

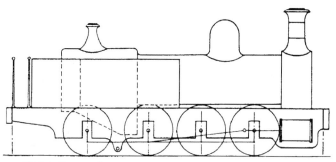

From an official diagram]
Vale of Neath Railway 0-8-0T Nos. 22/23 (G.W.R. Nos. 415/6)
Built by Slaughter, Gruning & Co., 1864

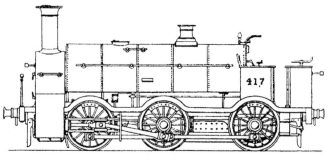

Vale of Neath Railway 0-6-0T No. 24
As G.W.R. No. 417
Built Vulcan Foundry, 1865

VNR Locomotives.

RCTS GW Locomotives Part 3.

Chapter 3
THE STANDARD GAUGE

Key NAH Personnel:

William Fitzmaurice M.P.	Chairman
The Chisholm	Deputy Chairman
Joseph Robinson	Deputy Chairman
Thomas Brown	Shareholder, Director
Charles Liddell	Engineer
Richard Moon	LNWR-nominated Director
Henry Tootal	LNWR-nominated Director
William Price M.P.	Director, later Chairman
Percy Morris	General Manager
Henry Griffiths	Station Master, Pontypool Rd.
Thomas Pritchard	Secretary
Mark Carr	Resident Engineer

The Newport, Abergavenny and Hereford was similar to the Vale of Neath in one respect; both were railways initially destined for Merthyr which turned their prime focus towards Aberdare. In other respects they were very different and, unlike the Vale of Neath, the Newport, Abergavenny and Hereford was an English company. It was formed on 24 April 1845 with its first office at 65 Moorgate in the City of London, the office of the solicitors, Johnston, Farquhar and Leech. The Head Office was to remain in London until 1858. The first Chairman was John Chapman; he and the other Directors all had London addresses.

The objectives of the Company, as set out in a prospectus, were to link the Midlands with the mineral production of Monmouthshire, and with Cardiff and Merthyr, and to provide new markets for the agricultural products of Herefordshire; reference was made to a Board of Trade memo which argued the importance of a chain of communication and the need not only for a broad gauge line along the south Wales coast to London, but also for a standard gauge line from south Wales to Birmingham. The general preamble bore a marked resemblance to the prospectus of another company formed about the same time called the Welsh Midland Railway (WMR). The NAH proposed to reach Merthyr by a branch line from Abergavenny by way of Brecon while another branch from Abergavenny to Monmouth was seen as a contribution to the grand plan of the Welsh Midland to build a railway from Worcester to Hereford, Brecon, and Carmarthen, with a branch from Brecon to

NAH Coat of Arms, from panel of First Class Carriage.

WIMM: GW Coll.

NAH Common Seal.

WIMM: GW Coll.

Merthyr, thence by way of the Taff Vale to Cardiff. In the NAH prospectus there was also reference to their objectives being helped by the existence of a railway from Merthyr to Cardiff. At this stage, access to Merthyr was envisaged by way of Brecon, not from Pontypool.

Tickets

Malcolm James Coll.

Pontypool Road West Junction, looking east; the lines to the left led to the NAH main-line at Pontypool Road Station South Junction; those to the right gave access to the vast complex of sidings.

R. H. Marrows.

From a very early stage relations with the Welsh Midland were fairly close. Activity must have been intense because on 22 May the board decided to negotiate the purchase of the MRCC as part of a thrust westward from Pontypool to Pontllanvrath (*sic*). This was the first reference to the idea of the NAH tapping the mineral resources of Monmouthshire by way of a line from Pontypool. At a meeting with the board of the WMR on 11 June, the NAH Board discussed the purchase of the Monmouthshire Canal Co. for £528,637. To this end the NAH muscled in on a company rather confusingly called the Monmouthshire Railway, originally formed as the Newport and Nantyglo Railway by a group of disaffected canal customers, with the aim of acquiring the assets of the MRCC (at that time still called the Monmouthshire Canal Co); these assets included authority to build the railway from Newport to Pontypool, then being processed in Parliamentary Committee. The purchase of the MRCC was eventually to be agreed and a deposit of £20,000 paid, but unfortunately for the NAH, the financial situation was to prevent its completion. Indeed financial pressures seem to have frustrated the efforts of the NAH from the start; even the £35,000 deposit payable to Parliament on submitting the NAH Bill had to be borrowed from the Cornwall and Devon Central Railway Company.

The westward extension from Pontypool then being actively considered would enable the NAH to link with existing tramways which ran down the valleys along its route. The first was the MRCC which occupied the Eastern and Western valleys of Monmouthshire. Down the Sirhowy valley the Sirhowy Tramway carried iron from Tredegar to the Monmouthshire Canal. It had been created by Act of Parliament in 1802 and functioned by private carriers operating their own trains against payment of a toll. In 1860 it was to become a railway. In the interim the track was progressively improved to meet increasing demands, and as early as 1829, the first steam locomotive was in operation. The third tramway, the Rumney (*sic*), ran down the Monmouthshire side of the Rhymney valley. The NAH were to endeavour to purchase it, and indeed terms were agreed, but when it came to finalising the deal, the money, once again, could not be found. In retrospect neither the MRCC nor the Rumney was of strategic importance to the goal of moving Welsh minerals to the Midlands and, given the financial constraints, the NAH would have been advised at this early stage to have focussed on what was to be the Taff Vale Extension, tapping the tramways but not owning them.

In the autumn of 1845 the NAH directors came under heavy pressure from their competitors; on 29 September a public meeting in Abergavenny (chaired by the Vicar) heartily endorsed the plan of the GE&W to build a broad gauge railway linking the Vale of Neath to what in 1851 was to be called the Hereford, Ross & Gloucester Railway, by way of Abergavenny. In October, Parliament authorised the MRCC line from Newport to Pontypool; as a result, the town of Newport—prominent in the NAH title—was never to be reached other than by way of running powers. At the northern end of the line, the WMR were trying to persuade the NAH to drop their plans beyond Abergavenny and to give up Hereford altogether. It is hardly surprising that the NAH declined this proposal, feeling uncomfortable with the threat of being squeezed into the space between Pontypool and Abergavenny.

Then the tide began to turn, for by December 1845, the WMR had run into difficulty, having failed to get their plans before Parliament in good order. The deadline for the submission to Parliament had been 30 November 1845 during which month the engineer engaged to prepare the plans and sections for the Bill, one Sydney Hall, was taken ill; when he recovered, he discovered that the drawings, which by then had been submitted to Parliament, were faulty. Leave was therefore sought from the House of Commons Committee to resubmit them. The case was referred to the Standing Order Committee, but Parliament appears not to have been moved.

As an alternative to making their own approach to Parliament, the WMR sought unsuccessfully to ride on the back of the NAH and to get the capital of the two companies

merged. In January 1846 the WMR was still sufficiently alive for the NAH to be talking again of amalgamation as part of a tri-partite merger to include also the MRCC. This unlikely union was never consummated; the MRCC was too poor and in any case had a vested interest in traffic not being syphoned off the valley tramroads by the line from Pontypool. Thereafter the WMR directors seem to have run out of ideas, and by June had decided to dissolve the company. A reconstituted successor was in no position to object when on 30 June the NAH made a new alliance, this time with the GE&W, whose engineer had also had difficulty meeting Parliamentary deadlines. In return for support in Parliament, the NAH were to agree to a merger with the GE&W and to include in their Bill a line from Abergavenny to Merthyr, thence to Hirwaun to join the proposed Vale of Neath; this alliance appears rather surprising because the GE&W was already in bed with the Vale of Neath which was to be incorporated just over one month later as a broad gauge railway. Perhaps it was a ploy by the NAH to neutralise the broad gauge party, as they may have assessed that the gauge would be critical and in their favour. Nevertheless the *Railway Times* judged the deal with the NAH to be attractive for the GE&W shareholders. In return for the activity by the NAH in Parliament, the GE&W would jointly finance the line from Pontypool to Hereford. The WMR were to be a third partner if they could raise the capital. This they failed to do and amid widespread recrimination the company was dissolved again.

Whatever the merits of the Great Eastern and Western, whether as ally or rival to the NAH, Parliament passed the NAH Act on 6 August 1846, three days after the Vale of Neath. The NAH, having for a year wantonly moved from one embrace to another, emerged independent but poor. The Act dismissively referred to the GE&W duplicating the NAH proposal and entitled its shareholders to convert to the NAH, which was now authorised to build a railway from Hereford to a junction at Pontypool with the already authorised Newport to Pontypool line of the MRCC; there were other branches to the east in Monmouthshire, but there was no mention

VNR eight-coupled haulage: an impression of how Neath High and Low Level Stations might have appeared ca. 1867.

GBJ

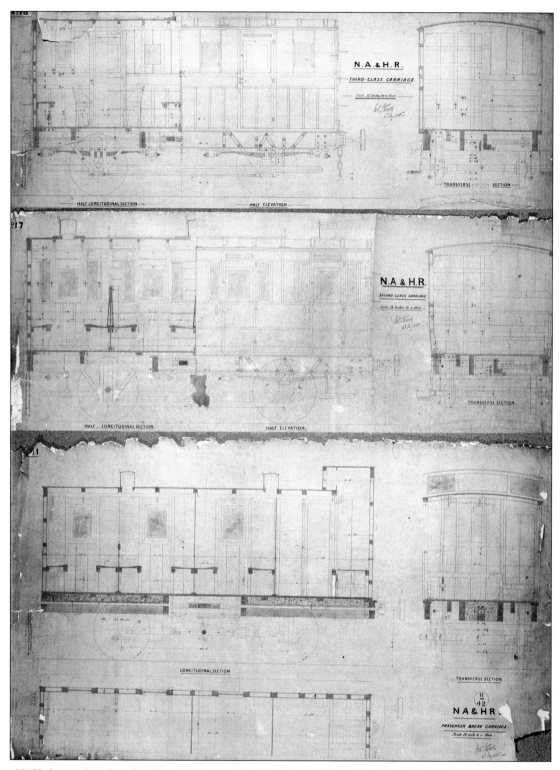

NAH plans and section of rolling stock prepared by Sturrocks and signed by Richard Sturrock 4th January 1855.
(*see page 80*).

ANNO DECIMO & UNDECIMO

VICTORIÆ REGINÆ.

****

Cap. clxxvii.

An Act to enable the *Newport, Abergavenny, and Hereford* Railway Company to extend their Railway from the Neighbourhood of *Pontipool* to the *Taff Vale* Railway. [9th *July* 1847.]

WHEREAS by the *Newport, Abergavenny, and Hereford* Railway Act, 1846, a Company was incorporated by the Name or Style of "The *Newport, Abergavenny, and Hereford* Railway Company," for making a Railway from *Newport* to *Abergavenny* and *Hereford*, with Branches therefrom : And whereas it is expedient that the *Newport, Abergavenny, and Hereford* Railway Company should be authorized to make a Railway from the Southern Terminus of their proposed Main Line in the Parish of *Llanvrechva Upper* in the County of *Monmouth* to join the *Taff Vale* Railway in the Parish of *Merthyr Tydvil* in the County of *Glamorgan*, near *Quakers Yard*: And whereas it is also expedient that some of the Powers and Provisions of the said recited Act should be amended and enlarged; but the Purposes aforesaid cannot be effected without the Authority of Parliament: May it therefore please Your Majesty that it may be enacted; and be it enacted by the Queen's most Excellent Majesty, by and with the Advice and Consent of the Lords Spiritual and Temporal, and Commons, in this present Parliament

[*Local.*]   26 K

9 & 10 Vict c. 303.

The TVE Act of Parliament, page 1.
House of Lords Record Office.

of the NAH being obliged to take over the GE&W proposal to construct a line from Abergavenny to Hirwaun, nor was there any mention of the link from Pontypool to the Taff Vale. The railway was required to keep at least 15 ft away from the walls of Abergavenny Castle; otherwise the route northward was to be along three existing tramways which the NAH was authorised to purchase.

The Hon. William Fitzmaurice had become Chairman of the NAH on 1 May 1845. Born in 1805, the second son of Viscount Kirkwall, he had been a Captain in the Life Guards but was then an Army major; he was Conservative MP for Buckinghamshire from 1842 to 1847, and, unlike Villiers of the VNR, voted against the repeal of the Corn Laws. This appears to have cost him his seat. He said himself that he had travelled over three quarters of the world, and he seems to have been familiar with the Middle East. He was something of an artist, as he illustrated several books, including an edition of *Childe Harold*, and a book of *Bible* illustrations. From subsequent events, we can conclude that he was a modest, sensitive and likeable man, a diligent chairman, who travelled extensively in Monmouthshire to familiarise himself with the geography and the market, but was perhaps not as strong and visionary a leader as the NAH needed. He certainly lacked the connections of Villiers of the VNR. It is perhaps significant that it was the Deputy Chairman, The Chisholm, who made the last-minute and critical deal with the GE&W. However by the time the line was complete and running to Hereford and to the Taff Vale, he was considered so indispensable that he was persuaded to continue in office for another year, after first tendering his resignation in August 1858.

At the first board meeting after the Act was passed, it was resolved to proceed with the main line immediately. The NAH then set about preparing for two further Acts which were passed in 1847. The first on 2 July authorised further small branches to the main line, the second, on 9 July and entitled The Newport, Abergavenny and Hereford Railway (Extension to Taff Vale Railway) Act, authorised the construction of a railway from a junction with the NAH at Llanvrechva (*sic*) near Pontypool to a junction with the TVR in the Parish of Merthyr at Quakers Yard. Compulsory right of land purchase was granted for three years only and completion was to be in seven years. The original authorised capital of the company of £733,000 in 29,310 £25 shares was increased by £400,000. Both of the 1847 Acts referred specifically to the Gauge Act and to its applicability in this case.

The Taff Vale Extension (TVE) was of profound strategic importance to the NAH. A special report by an engineer, John Miller, commissioned to examine the project, stated that the TVE would be 'most important to the main undertaking and . . .embracing prospects rarely to be met with in a line of railway'. It is not altogether clear why the NAH took two bites at the cherry and did not include the TVE in its first Act; it may be that the topography of the route was discouraging; perhaps it was hard enough to

0-6-2T No. 6653 heads east from Crumlin Junction. May 1957.

John Hodge.

An early but undated view of Hafodyrynys Platform opened in 1913, looking towards the Ebbw Valley.

NMRW.

get the line to Hereford against the competition and in a state of financial weakness, but, with the benefit of hindsight, it does look as though a clear-sighted and determined leader could have seen the merit of a line from Quakers Yard to Hereford by way of Pontypool and Abergavenny in 1845.

The TVE was not even the first railway to be projected from Pontypool to the valley of the Taff, for in November 1845 plans and sections were registered at the county offices in Monmouth for a line westward from Pontypool called the Pontypool and Merthyr Tydvil (*sic*) Railway (PMT). Its route was similar to that which was eventually constructed, the main divergence being at the western end where the PMT route crossed the TVR Llancaiach branch to the south of Nelson, necessitating a bridge over the Taff before reaching the Taff Vale Railway, but its gradient profile was very different; for instance at Hafodyrynys a 1,364 yds tunnel led to a long slope down at 1 in 40 to a crossing of the Ebbw, which was to be over a single arched bridge only 20 ft above the river and 40 ft in length. Between the Ebbw and the Sirhowy there was to be another tunnel, of 400 yds, and the Rhymney was approached through a 1000 yds tunnel, leading to a crossing only 15 ft high. This suggests that the route had been influenced by a need to meet the valley tramroads as close as possible to the level of their track, rather than by a desire to achieve a moderate overall ruling gradient. It also reflects a marked preference for tunnelling over bridge building. The engineer responsible was the wretched Gravatt of the GE&W.

An eastbound train descends the Glyn Valley *en route* to Pontypool Road. August 1963.

Alan Jarvis.

0-6-2T No. 5647 shunts the sidings connecting the TVE with the Rhymney Railway, west of Hengoed High Level Station. December 1963.

John Davies.

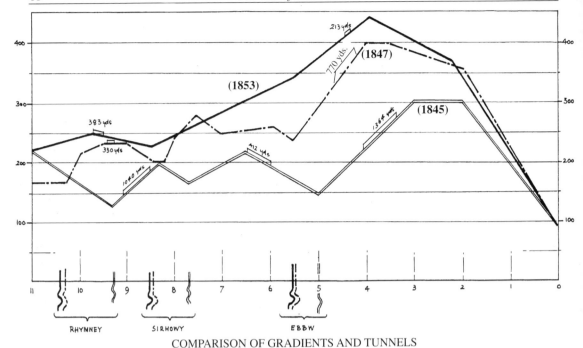

213 yds

(1847)

770 yds

(1853)

(1845)

383 yds

330 yds

1364 yds

1040 yds

412 yds

RHYMNEY   SIRHOWY   EBBW

COMPARISON OF GRADIENTS AND TUNNELS

The three lines illustrate how successive engineers eased the gradients for eastbound coal trains. The 1845 line shows how Gravatt was not averse to gradients or tunnels and more concerned to approach the levels of the various tramroads near the valley floors. In 1847 an appreciable effort was made to ease the crossing of the Ebbw and, in 1853, Liddell improved this further, as well as easing the crossings of both Rhymney and Sirhowy.
The varying distances to the river crossings reflect minor variations in the routes.

GBJ.

The biggest difference between the gradient profile of the line in the 1847 Act and that of the PMT was at Crumlin. From the east, at Hafodyrynys, it was possible to allow for a shorter tunnel of 770 yds and a shorter descent at 1 in 44 to the Ebbw, by providing a much bigger bridge 180 yards long and 117 ft high. There was debate about the effect of raising the height of the TVE, on the connections with the tramways along the valleys. Benjamin Hall argued that this problem was of minor significance since there was a natural gradient of 1 in 60 down the valleys; in practice the problem only arose on the Llanhilleth branch which involved a hard climb for loaded trains at 1 in 40.

Whether the PMT promotors had any connection with the NAH is unclear and there is no reference to the PMT in the NAH papers, but the similarity of the routes in a relatively small community would argue for some connection, and the fact that Gravatt was engaged as engineer to both the PMT and the GE&W suggests that

there was a link between those two companies. It would therefore seem likely that the drawings became available to the NAH as a result of the agreements made between them and the GE&W, and that they therefore represent the first drafting of the route of the eventual Taff Vale Extension.

The hearing by the Parliamentary committee of the evidence for and against the railway throws colourful light on local attitudes. The committee went into great detail to understand the economics of the projected line and called evidence from many people; a Merthyr brewer, mining engineers, surveyors, railway engineers, landowners, colliery owners, and a butcher from Merthyr who bewailed the current method of getting meat from Abergavenny market by driving it on foot 'upon the worst road even of any in Wales'. (Clearly Merthyr was surrounded by bad roads.)

But the traffic was not only to be in one direction; hay and beans for the pit ponies at Merthyr, and meat and vegetables from

Herefordshire were foreseen as an opportunity for the ballast run. Interrogated as to why the existing methods of transport were inadequate, the answers were powerful and sometimes colourful; one colliery owner, when asked why food produce for Merthyr could not be taken via Newport, Cardiff and the TVR, said, 'I don't know whether it is pretended it would be carried all along down to Newport, then along that half-yellow looking broad gauge line to Cardiff, and then to Merthyr.' In referring to the broad gauge as half-yellow he was probably referring to the colour of the ink on the map, but his tone was clearly uncomplimentary. Another witness, interested in getting coal and iron to the Midlands, complained specifically at the inconvenience of the break of gauge at Newport and Gloucester as being 'perfectly unprofitable.' Witnesses were equally uncomplimentary about shipping to Liverpool by sea, complaining of the extra working capital and the unreliability. In the House of Lords Committee it was also argued that carriage by sea caused rusting and deterioration of the bloom on the iron which was worth as much as £1 per ton.

After quite considerable Parliamentary expenditure of £12,693, the argument was eventually won and the project approved. The arguments of the ironmasters, the colliery owners and general tradesmen prevailed over those of the tramway and canal owners. However, by the end of 1847, the Repeal of the Corn Laws, the Irish famine and the aftermath of the Railway Mania conspired successively to ruin business confidence. In early 1848 the NAH, just like the Vale of Neath, applied to the Railway Commissioners for permission to extend the deadlines for land acquisition and completion by two years. This was approved in February 1849. The deadline for completion of the TVE was extended to July 1856. Then, unlike the VNR, the NAH directors appear to have decided to do nothing until the financial climate improved. They agreed to reduce their annual fees from £800 to £400 and the Company Secretary took a cut in salary from £600 to £400. The next General Meetings had little substance as there was little activity to report. Indeed, three meetings in 1849, 1850 and 1851 were aborted

for lack of a quorum. Towards the end of 1847, the contractor for the main line was approached with a view to securing a delay in construction. The Midland Railway was approached for assistance but to no avail due to the absence of any physical connection, especially between Worcester and Hereford. In November 1848 a postponement until 1851 of the purchase of the three tramways was negotiated, and in April 1850 John Chapman, the first chairman, resigned from the board.

Then in 1851 evidence of competitive activity caused the NAH to bestir itself. To the west, the VNR, having persevered through the bad times, was able to open its broad gauge line from Neath to Aberdare. To the east the GWR was threatening the standard gauge in the area of Birmingham and even looked as though it would reach the Mersey at Birkenhead, and in 1853 the Hereford, Ross and Gloucester was constituted as a broad gauge protégé of the GWR. A report to the NAH shareholders on 20 May urged the resumption of work. The construction of the vital link over standard gauge lines to Birmingham and the north of England, represented by the Shrewsbury & Hereford, now seemed certain. Without such a link, the NAH was without purpose, but competitive access to the Midlands also required a link from Hereford across to Worcester; this was destined to take an exasperating ten years to complete.

Besides being vulnerable strategically, the NAH was still financially weak. After six years it still had no income, and inactivity had caused a number of shareholders to default, such that 6,031 shares out of the 22,220 registered were in arrears. However a major clean-out of defaulting shareholders was achieved in 1851, and new shareholders were acquired, mainly business men from Abergavenny, but also two key figures (Brown and Robinson) from the Ebbw Vale Iron Co. Significantly the LNWR took the opportunity to take a small stake. In fact 1,940 shares were bought in the name of individual members of the management such as Huish, Moon and Tootal, and sent to Charles Stewart, the LNWR secretary, though who actually paid for them is not revealed. The new shareholders were given to expect that only £17 10s. 0d. of each £25 share would need to be called to complete the main line.

Simultaneously the number of directors was increased from 5 to 15, with a notable influx of local businessmen, including the aforementioned Brown, and Robinson who became Deputy Chairman; three were from Hereford, and Blake, Carnegie and Moon were from the LNWR. In January, Carnegie was replaced by Edward Tootal, another director of the North Western, which still held the key to English markets; with the difficulties in getting a line from Hereford to Worcester, access to these markets was then dependent on the opening of the line from Hereford to Shrewsbury. Pressing on to the Taff and tapping the coal seams of Monmouthshire and Glamorgan was vital, indeed arguably the main *raison d'être* for the NAH, so it was decided to accelerate matters by looking to the standard gauge allies for help.

While the Great Western was planning a broad gauge line from Worcester to Hereford, efforts to progress a standard gauge line were being made by the LNWR and the Midland. Accordingly in March 1851 the NAH board agreed to approach both these companies, emphasising the key position of the NAH as a potential standard gauge line, beset by the broad gauge party, who, it was argued, were seeking to monopolise the trade between south Wales and the north of England. The NAH proposed that the three parties share the investment of £300,000 in an extension of the NAH to Worcester, the whole to be operated by the Midland and LNWR. Discussions with the North Western concluded with agreement that the two companies should merge, once the Worcester and Hereford (W&H) was complete. In a so-called Supplemental Agreement, the LNWR undertook to operate the NAH from Newport to Hereford once that line was completed and until the opening of the Worcester and Hereford. The NAH was to receive each half year £10,000 from the gross receipts plus costs of rates, repairs and taxes; the LNWR was to receive working expenses, and interest on capital; both would share the surplus profit. The whole was to take effect once the W&H was authorised. When a bill reached Parliament the following year for such a standard gauge line from Worcester to Hereford, it was defeated in the Lords at the behest of the GWR and the Shrewsbury & Hereford. A year later, in 1853, it was submitted again, simultaneously with a rival broad gauge scheme. This time it was passed, though the House of Lords insisted that the LNWR should have no role in its affairs. This was damaging for the NAH as it removed the principle source of finance for the line and was to cause a serious delay in its construction, a revised Bill not being ready until 1858.

On the recommendation of the Cardwell Committee of the Board of Trade, the application for a merger of the NAH and LNWR was withdrawn in February 1853. Parliament was fearful of monopolies and was particularly suspicious of the North Western, whose recent application to merge with the Midland had been regarded as grotesque. In spite of these setbacks, the LNWR agreed to maintain the agreement to operate the NAH once open. Presumably to keep a foot in the door, and in order to assist the NAH finance its Taff Vale Extension, the LNWR made a second Supplemental Agreement, extending the operating agreement to the TVE on condition that it was open as far as Crumlin by July 1854.

In 1852 the LNWR had carried out a market study of south Wales, and, as the eventual take-over of the Sirhowy Railway and the as yet undreamed of Merthyr, Tredegar and Abergavenny (MTA) were to demonstrate, the prize was clearly seen to be attractive. This study by Moon and Tootal, which was more of an argument for territorial aggression than a well substantiated economic case based on market analysis, was contained in a memorandum to the LNWR board dated 9 October 1852. It argued as follows:

1. The broad gauge was threatening Birmingham, Birkenhead and Lancashire.
2. The TVE was likely to be complete by the middle of 1854.
3. A number of independent and isolated narrow gauge lines to the Welsh ports already existed; these could be linked with the LNWR and the Midland's 1,200 miles of track in England for the price of 43 miles of track at £10,000 a mile.

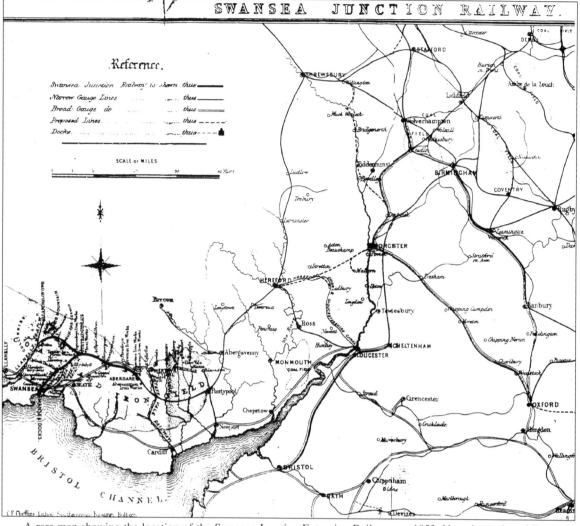

A rare map showing the location of the Swansea Junction Extension Railway ca. 1853. Note the projected line from Abergavenny to Brecon.

WIMM.

4. The landowners in the form of the Duke of Beaufort and the Marquis of Bute, hitherto broad gauge allies, were keen to get narrow gauge links.

5. There was a threatened broad gauge line from the Hereford, Ross and Gloucester to the mixed OWW and the VNR at Merthyr.

6. It was therefore necessary to act quickly.

7. Losing the Worcester & Hereford in Parliament enhanced the need to thwart the GWR.

8. 4 million tons of minerals per annum were being produced in south Wales.

In July 1852, with LNWR encouragement, the board of the NAH resolved to extend the TVE westward beyond Quakers Yard to Aberdare, thence to Swansea by means of a northward loop, which would avoid tangling with the Vale of Neath in Aberdare.

The line of this proposed railway is of interest and importance to the rest of this story. From Quakers Yard it was to cross the TVR and Taff river by a viaduct and then enter a tunnel under the mountain called Cefn Glas; when it emerged in the Aberdare valley it was to cling to the hillside above Aberdare and only come close to the line of the VNR at Hirwaun. From a point close to the Pencaedrain tunnel on the VNR it turned north before describing a great curve across the high ground and descending to Swansea along the Tawe valley. A branch dropped from near the Cefn Glas tunnel to the floor of the Cynon valley below Middle Duffryn. A year later in 1855 this location was to feature again in an Act authorising an extension of the VNR by the Aberdare Valley Railway.

The Swansea Junction Extension Bill was rejected; this, the third rejection by Parliament, must have added to the growing LNWR disenchantment with the NAH as a vehicle for achieving its ambitions in south Wales. The reasons for Parliament's rejection are not totally clear; the *Railway Times* considered the project of no merit until the W&H was completed; the House of Commons Committee was exercised by the rate of progress on the NAH main line, by the fact that decisions had been taken not to proceed with two branches from that main line without going back to Parliament, and by the discrepancy between the originally forecast cost of the main line and its eventual much lower cost. J. Palmer Budd who had been Deputy Chairman of the failed WMR and, since 1851, a director of the NAH, said rather smugly under cross-examination in committee, 'They did a great many foolish things before I joined them.'

For the NAH the importance of the Swansea Junction Extension Bill was that it introduced the subject of Aberdare, and placed the idea of extending west from Quakers Yard to tap the massive reserves of steam coal in the Cynon Valley firmly on the table. This was to become of prime strategic importance once it was realised that locomotives could be fired sufficiently cleanly on this coal without having to rely on coke. From August 1854, Richard Moon withdrew from the NAH board, one month after the NAH failed to meet the deadline for reaching Crumlin. Only Tootal remained and he was to prove an active and useful member of sub-committees, right to the end. In 1854 the NAH and LNWR agreed once more to promote a Bill for merger, but yet again it failed. In 1855 came the final blow when Parliament refused a request by the LNWR for reconsideration of the ban on

its involvement with the W&H; this appears to have put an end to the North Western's already dwindling interest in NAH affairs.

Meanwhile, stimulated at last to make some positive moves, the construction of the Main Line from Pontypool to Hereford had been receiving some attention. On 16 April 1851, the board resolved to instruct the engineer to lay out the line from Abergavenny to Hereford using the existing tramways as far as possible. Later in the year the contractor, Rennie, who had been the victim of the previous delay, was given the go-ahead.

By the middle of 1852 the limit of the work on the TVE was the steep-sided valley of the river Ebbw which Coxe had admired in 1799. In July the board received a report from the newly appointed Engineer, Charles Liddell, on Thomas Kennard's plan to build an iron girder bridge. They then moved uncharacteristically fast, and demonstrated qualities quite out of keeping with their previous style: courage, foresight, vision and decisiveness. In August the board decided to invite tenders, and by October they had received two, one for what was described as a lattice bridge, the other from Kennard of Falkirk. He was awarded the contract to build the Crumlin Viaduct. The contract for the line as far as the viaduct had been let to Rennie, and as soon as the contract to build the viaduct had been signed, the Engineer was instructed to call tenders for the continuation of the line westward to the Taff.

Thus by the end of 1852 much was at last happening. Fresh attention was also being paid to the links that could be made with tramways crossing the line of the TVE and a further Act of Parliament was passed in 1853 (the NAH [TVE] Act) to authorise such links with the Monmouthshire Railway at Llanhilleth, just east of the Crumlin Viaduct; with the Sirhowy Tramway at Pontllanfraith, and with the Rhymney Railway (RR) at Hengoed. Originally it had been intended to build a link with the Old Rumney Tramway along the bottom of the valley on the Monmouthshire side of the Rhymney river, but the quality of the track prohibited interchange. The arrival in 1854 of the Rhymney Railway, running on the other side of the river, at a higher level, enabled Liddell to achieve the ultimate easing of the gradients. Whereas the Rhymney river was originally to be crossed at a height of only 15 ft, involving a gradient down from the watershed of 1 in 44, Liddell inserted the Hengoed viaduct, 130 ft high. The height of the Crumlin Viaduct was raised still further to 200ft which increased the length to 500 yds. Further easing of the gradients, thus raising again the overall height of the line, was probably even more desirable with the development of the plans to extend into the Aberdare valley, which would increase the eastward movement of loaded coal trains. Minor alterations were made to the route, most obviously at Pontllanfraith, where the crossing of the Sirhowy river was located north rather than south of the village.

By the time the 1853 Act was passed, the contract for the Crumlin Viaduct had been let to Kennard, notwithstanding the fact that the plans and sections prepared for Parliament assumed an arched stone or brick viaduct over the Ebbw. It is not clear what caused this change of design. It has been argued that, in the narrow steep-sided

valley, a solid bridge would be exposed to strong lateral forces from the wind, and that this alone would justify an iron girder construction, but it seems more likely to have been on grounds of cost.

The LNWR was still committed to operating the NAH mainline when it opened. In September 1853 Huish, the mercurial manager of the LNWR, had travelled the length of the line from Hereford to Pontypool and had commented favourably upon it. Opening was planned for 6 December 1853 and celebrations were held, but a bad landslip in a deep cutting just north of Abergavenny, at the top of the Llanfihangel bank, delayed actual opening until 2 January 1854. The good news was that the Shrewsbury & Hereford opened on 6 December, at last linking the NAH to the rest of the standard gauge system. At this point, ideally, the TVE should also have been ready, but four years were to pass before the vital link between the coalfields and the Midlands was completed.

Crumlin Viaduct seen from the drive up to Crumlin High Level Station in June 1964.

J. Stone.

Charles Liddell in 1894.   Tom Kennard in 1893.

ILN.   *ILN.*

Crumlin Junction looking west in 1906; the Llanhilleth Branch drops away to the right.

WIMM: GW Coll.

Crumlin Junction looking towards Hafodyrynys. June 1963.

R. H. Marrows.

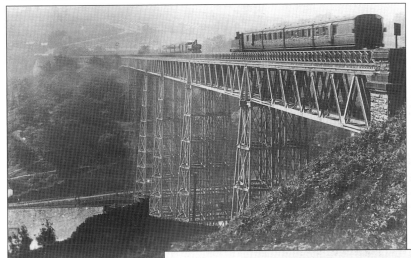

During double track days—two trains crossing the Crumlin Viaduct.

R. H. Marrows Coll.

Looking eastward at Crumlin Viaduct and Junction, showing the Llanhilleth Branch coming in from the left. No date.

WIMM: GW Coll.

Llanhilleth Colliery, with the branch from Crumlin Junction in the immediate foreground. Compare this scene of industrial activity with the tranquillity of the old church yard illustrated on page 14.

John Cornwell.

West portal of Bryn Tunnel. July 1965.
R. H. Marrows.

East portal of Bryn Tunnel from the footplate.
Wayne Hopkins.

Sawing timber for the nearly-completed Crumlin Viaduct. 1857.
NMRW.

A carefully posed photograph on Crumlin Viaduct showing the original wood decking before a rail was laid. The confident figure with a cigar in his hand, standing in the foreground, could well be Tom Kennard. 1857.

NMRW.

During 1854, work on the TVE was intensified. The steep climb up the Glyn valley from Pontypool westward was eased and the Blaendare Tramway which ran parallel part of the way up the valley was bought to increase eventual capacity; this was later known as 'the third line'. On the other side of the Crumlin Viaduct, bores were being sunk to prepare for the Bryn Tunnel through the watershed between the Rhymney and Sirhowy rivers. In October 1855, over one year after the deadline set in the Supplemental Agreement with the LNWR, the first stretch of line was opened from Pontypool as far as the Crumlin Viaduct, together with the branch to the MRCC at Llanhilleth. The forging of this link was not without opposition, not from the Board of the MRCC, but from its local engineer who tried to prevent the NAH from gaining physical access by removing the points. Relations with the MRCC were clearly uneasy as Professor Gordon, Liddell's partner, was told by Kennard that the MRCC were threatening to destroy his appliances if work on the Crumlin Viaduct were to proceed. In spite of local rivalry however, the Llanhilleth link appears to have been very busy from the start, with traffic in both directions. By May 1856, congestion on the Monmouthshire Railway northward up the Ebbw valley was such that the NAH was seeking the right to operate its own trains over the MRCC. The newly appointed station master at Pontypool, Henry Griffiths, claimed to the General Purpose Commitee of the Board that he was spending most of his time organising trains between Pontypool and Llanhilleth.

Pontypool Clarence Street looking east in 1963. The perspective of the station sign indicates the severity of the descent to Pontypool Road.
R. H. Marrows.

Maesycwmmer Junction looking west; the line to the right dropped away sharply to join the Brecon and Merthyr. April 1963.
R. H. Marrows.

An impressive study of the Hengoed Viaduct, with the Brecon & Merthyr line in the foreground, and the High
Level Station in the distance.

WIMM: GW Coll.

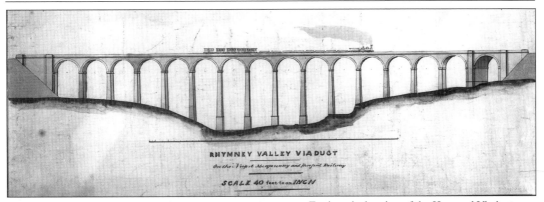

RHYMNEY VALLEY VIADUCT

On the Tredegar Abergavenny and Newport Railway

SCALE 40 feet to an INCH

Engineer's drawing of the Hengoed Viaduct over the Rhymney river. 1857.

PRO: Rail 513.16.

The skewed arch in the Hengoed Viaduct, constructed thus to accommodate the old Rumney Tramway, later the Brecon and Merthyr Railway. April 1963.

R. H. Marrows.

2-6-2T No. 4169 about to enter Hengoed High Level station with a westbound train. No date.

R. E. Toop.

Engraving of the opening of the Crumlin Viaduct, 1857.

ILN.

In 1857, the Crumlin Viaduct was eventually ready for the Government Inspector. The Llanhilleth branch was also tested and passed for use by passenger trains, subject to the insertion of a guard rail on the curve. Although later used for workmen's trains, this branch never became a regular passenger line.

With great celebrations the viaduct was opened officially on 1 June 1857, nearly five years from the start. The railway could then be opened to Tredegar Junction at Pontllanfraith, and was expected to be ready to Quakers Yard by the end of August; only the Rhymney viaduct and the Bryn tunnel remained incomplete, the viaduct being delayed by a strike of the stone masons. In June 1857 Liddell was commissioned to design a station at Crumlin with booking office, ladies waiting room and refreshment room, and bedrooms on the first floor, though his plans for an accompanying hotel were rejected.

A month later, negotiations began with the Taff Vale Railway. The TVR were basically well-disposed to the NAH which offered an end to their isolation from the standard gauge lines in the rest of the country. They had therefore been accommodating about the slippage in meeting the Parliamentary deadline of July 1856, for exercising rights of way at both Llancaiach and Quakers Yard. Negotiations covered access to Aberdare as well as traffic rights to Merthyr, in anticipation of completion to Quakers Yard. However, the TVR were unwilling to allow the NAH to run trains through to Merthyr for as long as their own line was only single track, though agreement was reached on the operation of the junction station at Quakers Yard. The NAH were to man the station but not the signalling. Just two passenger trains a day were to be permitted to Merthyr, with through booking of passengers and goods from Hereford to Merthyr, Dowlais, and Aberdare.

Finally on 5 January 1858 the TVE was opened to Quakers Yard, after a further delay had been caused by the inspector requiring some signalling modifications at Llancaiach. There had also been some problems with one of the company's shareholders who had obstructed progress. The nature of this obstruction is not

GWR eight-coupled haulage: No. 97, prototype of the 2800 class, portrayed at Quakers Yard ca. 1905.

GBJ

LNWR eight-coupled haulage: Bird-in-Hand Junction portrayed in the early days of the LMS, 1923.

Crumlin High Level looking west, with coal train headed by 0-6-0PT No. 3683. 16 April 1963.
R. H. Marrows.

Pontllanfraith Low Level Station looking west towards three bridges: the station foot-bridge, the road bridge and the LNWR bridge carrying the Sirhowy branch. June 1963.
R. H. Marrows.

A rare photograph of the railway bridge over the Sirhowy River. No date.
Wayne Hopkins Collection.

On a rural stretch of the line, 0-6-2T No. 5698 heads a Pontypool Road train between Penalltau Junction and Hengoed. No date.

Alan Jarvis.

Quakers Yard Low Level, originally Quakers Yard Junction, where the TVE joined the Taff Vale Railway.

Alan Jarvis.

A 5600 class 0-6-2T, heading a Merthyr-bound excursion, on the former TVR main-line, negotiates the junction with the TVE made in 1857 at Quakers Yard, while a pannier tank heads from the High Level station towards Cefn Glas Tunnel and Aberdare. 2 May 1964.

R. H. Marrows.

A general view of the junction between the TVE and the TVR with a 5600 class locomotive and van about to leave the TVE and pass the attractive little TVR box. 23 July 1960.

M. Hale, courtesy S. G. Whittaker.

revealed, but after so many delays it would be more natural for the shareholders to be impatient to start operations; it may therefore have been a shareholder who had a bigger stake in the MRCC, the Sirhowy, or the Rhymney, and resented the prospect of traffic being syphoned on to the TVE.

Carr, the Resident Engineer, reported the following works in hand at the start of 1858:

— Locomotive stables and store sheds (locomotives were still thought of as iron horses)

— Doubling track Pontypool to Crumlin

— Sidings at Crumlin

— 40 ft turntable at Quakers Yard (pending one at Merthyr)

— Points and crossings TVE

— Temporary stations Rhymney Jc. and Quakers Yard (the latter presumably while the Taff Vale were building their more permanent structure)

— Asphalting Crumlin Viaduct (presumably to protect the decking)

— Replacing Barlow rail (the whole NAH was originally laid with this unsatisfactory system)

— Station approach Pontypool Rd. (this and the former station master's house can still be seen in 1996, south of the road bridge over the railway)

— Station approach and sidings Pontypool (the approach road and a short length of platform are all that remain of Clarence Street in 1996).

However, this progress was not made without financial strain, which had been felt as early as November 1854. Less than a year from the opening to Hereford, the shareholders were receiving a report in somewhat defensive language. The LNWR was not, it was felt, fulfilling its obligations in operating the line, as inadequate locomotive capacity was hampering the development of trade. Attempts to set up a joint Traffic Committee to stimulate business were rebuffed by the LNWR as interference. When the Chairman wrote to Lord Chandos about it, the response was that perhaps the agreement should be terminated. The NAH problem was that under LNWR management, the Shrewsbury & Hereford was taking £16 per mile per week, whereas the NAH was only taking £10; even the MRCC between Newport and Pontypool was taking £22. The LNWR were also being greedy about the terms of transferring traffic over their system. Accordingly, the NAH decided to take over from 1 October 1854. It seems to have been an amicable settlement as the LNWR continued to loan vehicles, but only until April 1855, at which date they were summarily removed. This left the NAH unable to fulfil its obligations and losing trade until emergency replacements could be found. Furthermore Thomas Brassey, the famous contractor and supplier of hired locomotives to the LNWR, when sacked at the end of 1854, not only took away his engines, but removed all the equipment

from the workshop at Hereford as well. This all put pressure on profitability and funds. An E.G.M. called in November 1854 was informed that on top of the £17 10s. 0d. call previously predicted, a further £2 had been needed to cover the cost of linking to the S&H at Hereford, to the Clydach Tramway at Abergavenny, and the MRCC at Pontypool. After allowing a 3% dividend, it would be necessary to call the balance of £5 10s, 0d. on the existing £25 shares to complete the line to Crumlin, and then issue £100,000 in 5% preference stock to cover the cost of locomotives.

On 25 January 1855, tenders were accepted for the following rolling stock :

    4 1st class carriages at £285 each
    4 1st/2nd class carriages at £236
    6 2nd class carriages at £205
    8 3rd class carriages at £180
    4 passenger brake vans at £230
    4 horse boxes at £110
    4 carriage trucks at £65.

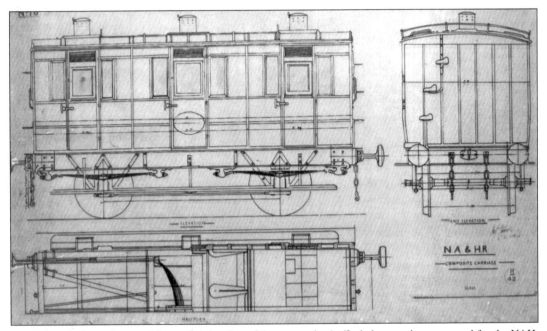

A computer-enhanced copy of Sturrocks' drawing of the composite 1st/2nd class carriage prepared for the NAH in January 1855.

An early 1920s view looking west from Hengoed High Level, showing, from the left, the Rhymney main-line to Ystrad Mynach, the Hengoed Loop by which the LNWR gained access from the TVE to the Rhymney, the TVE to Penalltau Junction, and the coal sidings.

WIMM: GW Coll.

In April, it was decided to order from Sturrocks of Doncaster 100 waggons at £78 each, capable when arranged in pairs of carrying up to 20 tons of rails or timber. These were to be supplied at the rate of 20 per week, the first batch being available within two weeks. Debate had covered the desirability of such a solution as compared with 50 six-wheel waggons at £130 each with a 16 ton capacity. It was felt that the price advantage of the latter would be outweighed by difficulties on curves and turntables and by the lower capacity.

Additional capital of £200,000 was now required to pay for the TVE. At an Extraordinary General Meeting on 19 July 1855, it was agreed to raise this £200,000 as 5% preference shares. Due to poor subscription, works had to be slowed. In March 1855 instructions were given that work on the Crumlin Viaduct and Bryn Tunnel were to be kept to a maximum of £1,000 per month, and on the line from Crumlin to the Sirhowy to £500; this inevitably delayed completion of the nearly finished Crumlin Viaduct. The Directors argued that, given the immense catchment area around Quakers Yard, a dividend of 6% should be certain. They quoted

the volume of coal being shipped from Cardiff and Newport—1½ million tons per annum—and mentioned the 132 blast furnaces in the area. An interesting comparison was made with the TVR, a company with an impeccable dividend performance, which was earning £90 per mile per week. In its second year of operation it had earned £20, whereas in the corresponding year the NAH had earned £21. Assuming an average cost of £20,000 per mile for building the rest of the TVE (total length 15 miles, i.e. £300,000), the directors felt that even at half the TVR rate of earning, i.e. £40, a return of 6% on the new capital was secure.

At the nineteenth Half-yearly General Meeting on 28 February 1856 the proposal to raise £200,000 in preference shares at up to 6%, convertible to ordinary shares at par, was accepted; but a sub-committee was set up to look more closely at the finances. At an Extraordinary General Meeting on 17 April 1856, this committee recommended increasing the capital by £350,000, £216,840 as 6% preference stock, the balance by debentures, in order to cover the cost of the extension of the TVE to Aberdare. They predicted earnings of £40 per mile per week, allowing 6% on the new shares. They emphasised the importance of the Aberdare market, and ended by recommending the appointment of two new Directors, to be 'gentlemen of business habits'. In May 1856 William Price M.P. became a director and immediately became very active. Born in Gloucester in 1817 he was a timber merchant and Liberal M.P. for Gloucester from 1852 to 1859 and 1865 to 1873. He was to succeed Fitzmaurice as chairman in 1859 and was later one of the Railway Commissioners.

Liddell Architecture I: Old Pontypool Road ca. 1908.

Torfaen Museum, Pontypool.

Liddell Architecture II: Pontllanfraith Low Level. June 1963.

R. H. Marrows.

Liddell Architecture III: Crumlin High Level. September 1960.

H. C. Casserley.

Liddell Architecture IV: Clarence Street, Pontypool. June 1964.

R. H. Marrows.

Liddell Architecture V: Old Llancaiach. No date.

Lens of Sutton.

Back in 1852, the Chairman had argued the holding of the Secretary's salary at £600, as he alone had kept the company together during a difficult time. This may be a pointer to the NAH weakness of inadequate management; they had no outstanding talent of the calibre of Joshua Williams of the VNR and it also looks as though too much was run from the London office. Percy Morris, the so-called General Manager, was clearly in a junior position and not blessed with the status or authority of Joshua Williams. Although he went on to the West Midland and later became General Manager of the North Staffordshire, he appears to have had much less grip on the company than Joshua Williams on the VNR. In practice the Chairman was involved in much of what should have been tackled by management. For example, even a reply from the G.M. in answer to a customer complaint required the Chairman's approval. Perhaps the Chairman felt more at ease dealing with the minutiae of the company's affairs than with strategy, the stock market and politics. Thomas Brown, a local entrepreneur, significant shareholder and NAH board member, when cross-examined in 1853 by Lord John Manners in connection with the application by the NAH to build the Swansea Junction Extension, said he had refrained from investing in the NAH at the beginning, as the estimated investment was too high. In response to the question, 'The NAH gave way to despair and abandoned their line?' he replied, 'They were unable to keep up the confidence with their proprietors and with the public to get it subscribed. The South Wales Railway had associated with gentlemen of great wealth. The Chairman Mr Talbot no doubt stuck to it so determinedly and energetically he mastered the difficulties.' By inference, the NAH chairman did not. Now, the secretary was not alone in being put under pressure; the General Manager was put on a performance related wage with a bonus of 2% of traffic proceeds up to £2,600 in a half year and 1% thereafter up to a maximum of £6,500. This was to be subject to revision, especially on the long awaited opening of the Worcester & Hereford. At the same time, as is frequently the case today, the need for a clarification of management roles was identified and so a redefinition of functions was put in hand.

To add to management's problems, there was a series of accidents. Today there is a widely accepted correlation between management quality and accident frequency, but to be fair to the NAH, in the middle of the last century, safety was not a management priority on any railway. On 12 November 1856, for example, there were two accidents: one at Pontypool Road, where some waggons from a MRCC train broke loose and were struck by a Newport to Hereford passenger train; the other more serious, between a goods train and a passenger train at Nantyderry, caused the death of two passengers. The driver of the goods train was convicted of manslaughter; in the evidence it transpired that he could neither read nor write and had been instructed in the rule book by his uncle and his cousin. In March 1859, again at Nantyderry, two boiler tubes in a goods engine burst killing two men and delaying a passenger train for 35 minutes. The accident cost the company £3292 5s. 11d. plus compensation to the families. In that same year there were a further three accidents in June, two more in August and three in September.

Meanwhile the financial position continued to cause concern and the directors required cost reductions and a monthly submission of accounts. The cost reductions were achieved primarily by reducing office staff, but inefficiencies were identified in the Engineer's department; in particular it was found that capital work, which should have been put out to tender, was being done in-house and put down as revenue. The sub-committee felt that the ultimate potential of the line as previously forecast was reasonable, but was concerned about short term profitability; the increase in earnings was unlikely to be sufficient to yield a dividend, so costs had to be taken out of the system. They envisaged that in the second half of 1857, £16,336 would be required to cover dividends and interest, but traffic receipts at £1,125 per week, less the expected 50% costs, would leave a shortfall of £1,711. In the half-year ending June 1858, dividend cover would require traffic of £1,430 per week if costs were not reduced.

The Company Secretary, Pritchard, received a drop in salary from £600 to £400 p.a. and an increase in responsibilities to include Purchases and Stores. Perhaps not altogether surprisingly, he retired in August, having been away ill. His place was taken by his deputy, Gordon Graham. At the end of the year the Deputy Chairman, Robinson, also retired. Within twelve months, all the key personnel who had been running the company from the early days had gone. As the following table shows, the management were able to take down costs to something approaching the national average, a commendable achievement in a recession caused by the Italian war :

NAH half-yearly traffic, in £'s

	Jun 1855	Dec 1855	Dec 1856
Pass.	6,227	8,602	9,353
Goods	6,144	6,564	12,074
Total	15,829	20,399	28,106
%costs	70.7	57.4	52.7

	Dec 1857	Dec 1858	Jun 1859
Pass.	10,397	12,425	10,207
Goods	12,879	14,523	13,673
Total	28,140	34,233	34,120
%costs	48.4	48.1	46.0

The results in 1859 were even more remarkable considering the fall in sales, attributable to the fact that the opening of the TVE coincided with a strike of colliers.

Now that the link to the TVR was in place, there were many operational developments during 1858. In January, the NAH agreed to run some locomotives over the Sirhowy Tramroad from Tredegar Junction down to Nine Mile Point, where the link was made with the MRCC; this was subject to first checking the curves in the track, and to the tramway agreeing to pay the cost of repairing any damage to the locomotives. In February, it was decided that six locomotives and guards' vans be fitted with a Great Northern type communication system, which was in fact no more sophisticated than a bell on the footplate connected by a continuous rope to the guard's position at the back of the train, but it was an important step. In April, the Rhymney Railway opened for traffic and, in May, an agreement on traffic handling was made with the Sirhowy Tramroad, which, until it became a railway, was to handle traffic from the NAH destined for Tredegar. Once it became a railway, the NAH reserved the right to opt to run its trains through from Tredegar to NAH destinations. The Sirhowy was to pay the cost of the new signalman at Tredegar Junction, though under the control of the NAH, and the new sidings installed at the junction would be removed if the tramroad did not become a railway within 18 months. In the same month, the NAH was complaining to the TVR that since the TVR had completed doubling the track to Merthyr and NAH locomotives were accordingly operating there, the small size of the turntable was necessitating the locomotives running tender first in one direction. The TVR were pressed to install a larger turntable. In September, Mr Jones the station master at Quakers Yard was reported to the Traffic Committee for inaccuracies in his accounts; he was to be permitted to tender his resignation, and the General Manager was authorised to accept it. In October, it was agreed that a small waiting shed for passengers be erected at Rhymney Junction (Hengoed) at a cost of £24. By the end of the year, the track had been doubled to Crumlin.

Goods traffic had clearly been generated in both directions; as early as April 1858, the VNR was noting that Merthyr coal trade with England was being diverted to the TVE. Other products were also moving; for instance flour from Chester to Merthyr, and rails from Llanhilleth to London, from Penydarren and Dowlais to East Retford, and from Quakers Yard to Cannock. In early 1860, agreement was made with the South Wales Railway to offer special rates for passengers travelling to Milford Haven for the Anglo-Luso Brazilian Steamers, provided through booking could be made from NAH stations. In May, a special excursion train from Ebbw Vale to Pontypool Rd. via the Llanhilleth curve was permitted. This is the first evidence of this line being used for passengers.

While the TVE was being completed the company had been preparing for the extension to Aberdare. At the end of 1856, solicitors were instructed to purchase land along the route and the board resolved to build through Middle Duffryn to 'the head of the Aberdare valley', to junctions with the Vale of Neath and the

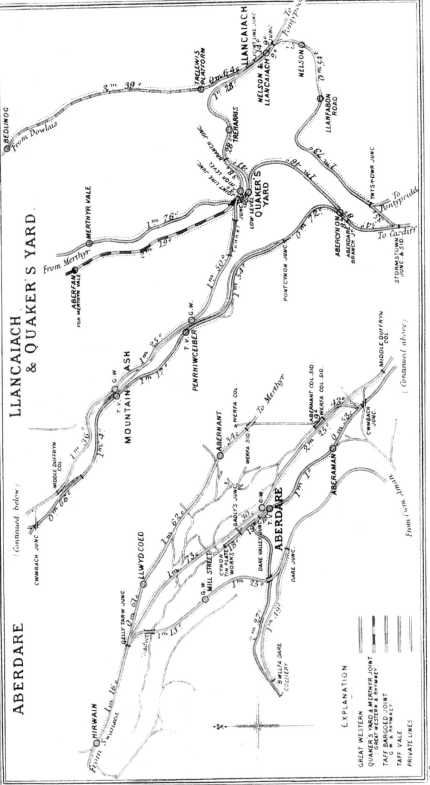

Railways in the Aberdare Valley, 1915.

Railway Clearing House.

Aberdare Railway (owned by the TVR). The exact nature of the end of the line was clearly undecided. The NAH and their successors, the West Midland Railway and eventually the GWR, played to keep their options open and competitors out. It also looks as though, at the latest by 1861, they had realised that the VNR had more at stake than they had, and could be allowed to make the running. The standard gauge TVR branch which left the main line up the Taff Vale at Navigation House (now Abercynon) ended in sidings, just beyond a station at Aberdare. The gauge suited the NAH, but the traffic potential was limited to the admittedly rich pickings of the Aberdare neighbourhood. The broad gauge VNR, on the other hand, reached Middle Duffryn in November 1857 and ran through Aberdare to Neath and Swansea, but

there was not yet any suggestion of mixing the gauge. Instead, in April 1857, Liddell reported to the board that a single NAH line alongside the VNR from Upper Duffryn to Aberdare would cost £8-9,000, whereas a single broad gauge line alongside the NAH from Middle Duffryn to Lower Duffryn would cost £3,300. A proposition to this effect was put to the VNR but seems to have been swamped by other pressures. In September 1857, the engineers were instructed to stake out the route for single and double track from Quakers Yard to Middle Duffryn and, by February 1858, this had been done, and sanction was given to take bore samples for the Cefn Glas tunnel and to start opening the cuttings; this part of the route was planned to be single track from the beginning; also that year an Act was obtained to divert the Aberdare canal.

Quakers Yard East Junction looking west; the original TVE bears left, down to the junction with the TVR; the line to the right is the later Aberdare extension, by way of Quakers Yard High Level and the Cefn Glas Tunnel. April 1964.

J. Stone.

Quakers Yard Low Level with its unusually long foot-bridge and low platform edge on the unused TVE side of the island platform. No 8717 simmers quietly.

David Lawrence, courtesy S. G. Whittaker.

A westbound train about to enter the eastern portal of Cefn Glas Tunnel. No date.

R. Roper, courtesy E. A. Evans.

The TVE viaduct over the Taff before subsidence caused timber support to be necessary.

WIMM: GW Coll.

NAH 2-4-0 locomotive, one of only four to be named on the NAH, built in 1855 by E. B. Wilson. The location is believed to be Ponthir Brickworks. No date.

Gwent Archives.

Report of the final meeting of the directors of the NAH, signed by W. P. Price, Chairman.

PRO: Rail 513.3

The NAH (Branches) Act of August 1857 authorised the NAH to construct an extension from Quakers Yard to the Aberdare valley, some four years after Parliament had rebuffed the Swansea Junction Extension railway. The new Act, besides authorising the link with the TVR, provided for a connection with the broad gauge VNR at Middle Duffryn, and also authorised the building of a line up the Bargoed Taff valley from what was later called Trelewis.

Following the 1857 Act, as part of the agreement with the TVR over rights to Merthyr and elsewhere, it was agreed that the NAH would operate between Middle Duffryn and the TVR station at Aberdare, through a link to be made between the NAH and the TVR at Mountain Ash. By the middle of 1858 tunnel shafts under Cefn Glas had been sunk and Liddell reported that the headings had penetrated

458 of the required 638 yards and that the viaduct across the Taff and a cutting were the only significant works outstanding. There was hesitation about engaging contractors because of the delicate financial position, but eventually this was done early in 1860, and the work was expected to be finished by May 1861.

It had been hoped that completion of the line to the Aberdare valley would coincide with the opening of the Worcester & Hereford, which eventually materialised in September 1861. However before that was achieved, managerial effort was absorbed in a series of mergers. In 1855 following the withdrawal of the LNWR from the agreements with the NAH, the Oxford, Worcester and Wolverhampton and the NAH had agreed on the benefits of the Worcester to Hereford link, and eventually made a pact to co-

Letter written shortly before the demise of the NAH by the Company Secretary to Francis Bodenham, a solicitor in Hereford who was one of the directors.

GBJ Coll.

operate, as though they were one company, each to contribute £25,000 in capital and to operate the W&H jointly in a 21 year contract. A revised Bill for the authorisation of the Worcester and Hereford Railway with the Midland Railway also as a partner was approved by Parliament in 1858 and work began. This co-operation led eventually to a proposal to amalgamate the OWW, the NAH and the Worcester and Hereford (but not the Midland); this was authorised by an Act of Parliament of July 1860, creating the West Midland Railway (West MR). Incidentally, this was not the first railway to be so called, for in 1845 a West Midland Railway had been projected from Crewe through the Potteries to Belper. The new company's Chairman was William Fenton of the OWW, with Price of the NAH as his deputy.

The Worcester & Hereford, which was once to have led the NAH into the arms of the LNWR, was now to accompany it into the rival camp, for in less than a year further amalgamation was in the air. On 30 May 1861, a special meeting of shareholders was called to consider the terms of the proposed merger of the West MR with the GWR. The basic proposition was that the GWR would take 82½% and the West MR 17½% of annual proceeds. Of this latter the OWW would take 78% and the NAH 22%, so the NAH became very much a minor party.

The operating results of the infant West MR were not encouraging. At the half-yearly meeting on 15 August 1861, it was reported that in the first half of the year, costs were up and proceeds down compared with both previous half years, part of the blame being placed on the exceptionally hard winter which had caused frost to damage the OWW's longitudinal sleepers. However, work on the Aberdare extension was then reported to be making rapid progress such that the line was expected be open by the end of the year. The financial results improved thereafter, but the E.G.M., called on 29 April 1863 to approve the Bill before Parliament, was decisively in favour of merger with the GWR.

Steam chiaroscuro. 0-6-2T No. 6622 emerges from the eastern portal of the Cefn Glas Tunnel with the 11.00 a.m. Aberdare to Pontypool Road train. 14 September 1963.

W. E. Spurrier, courtesy S. G. Whittaker.

Cefn Glas Tunnel, west portal. June 1963.
J. Stone.

Amidst this board room manoeuvring, it was thus the management of the West MR who, among their other cares, had taken over the responsibility for carrying the line westward through to Aberdare. Expected completion had slipped from May to year-end 1861 and was to slip still further. Clearly the nature of this link had continued to present a problem. In December 1859, the NAH board had still been discussing the possibility of granting the VNR access to Mountain Ash in return for access to their station at Aberdare. By the autumn of 1860, negotiations between the West MR and the VNR led to the concept of access to Neath and Swansea for the West MR provided the VNR put in a third rail; the West MR would pay 5% on the cost and grant the VNR access east of Middle Duffryn. The VNR response was positive but they were more concerned at this time with preventing a new standard gauge competitor gaining access to Swansea; their attention was focussed on the Swansea and Neath project

prompted by their desire to control the standard gauge access to Swansea. The Vale of Neath here missed an opportunity which was soon to disappear, for in a surprise move during 1861, the West MR sought to obtain authority to abandon the link to the VNR altogether. This put pressure on the VNR to convert to mixed gauge at their own expense.

At this point the GWR stepped into the picture. The West MR was projecting a new line from near Oxford to Knightsbridge in London called the London, Buckinghamshire and West Midland Junction Railway. Alarmed at this and the possibility of a standard gauge line to Swansea in the hands of the LNWR, who were on good terms with the West Midland, they acted quickly to amalgamate with both the SWR and the West MR, and thus keep the enemy out. This was achieved on 13 July and 1 August 1863 respectively. Meanwhile by an Act dated 29 July 1862, the VNR had obtained authority to instal a third rail. Under Heads of Agreement between the GWR and VNR dated 24 March 1863, as the price of VNR acquiescense in the merger with the South Wales, the GWR agreed to make the junction at Middle Duffryn (authorised by the NAH Act of 1857) and operate three trains a day in each direction between Swansea and Hereford. Through booking facilities were to be established by both companies and the VNR were to lay the third rail 'with all despatch'. This took place during 1863 but still in the summer of that year the West MR/GWR were hesitating; the GWR, having got control of the West MR and having thereby ensured that, if any standard gauge invasion was to occur, it would at least be able to control it, appeared in no particular hurry to reap the probably meagre rewards from Swansea. It was enough for the immediate future to be able to move coal from Mountain Ash. It has been argued that in any case the Cefn Glas tunnel was not ready until early 1864, yet this was never used as an excuse to the VNR and it seems more likely that, if it was still unfinished, it was because it was not yet needed. Meanwhile the frustrated Vale of Neath was urging that the link be completed and West Midland trains run into their Aberdare station rather than into that of the TVR. The first through goods train

A mineral train near Mountain Ash hauled by 2-6-2T No. 4136. March 1964.

G. T. Robinson.

A ballast train heads up the valley from Mountain Ash. May 1961.

GBJ.

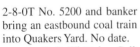

2-8-0T No. 5200 and banker bring an eastbound coal train into Quakers Yard. No date.

S. G. Whittaker Coll.

The 3.55 p.m. Pontypool Road to Neath train leaves Quakers Yard and enters the single line section through Cefn Glas Tunnel. 20 August 1962.

G. T. Robinson.

2-6-2T No. 4174 leaving the western portal of Cefn Glas Tunnel on the 2.25 p.m. Pontypool Road to Neath train, 13 March 1964.

G. T. Robinson.

eventually ran on 18 April 1864 and the first Hereford to Swansea through passenger train ran on 5 October. The link to the TVR authorised by the 1857 Act was eventually put in at Mountain Ash in 1864. The 1858 agreement with the TVR was to prove an expensive inheritance for the Great Western, when it finally selected the option of the link to Swansea via the VNR at Middle Duffryn; compensation had to be paid to the TVR on all passenger and goods traffic other than coal originating or terminating between Aberdare and Middle Duffryn and destined for, or derived from, an easterly direction.

The NAH emerges from the records as a company betraying many human frailties, vulnerable rather than confident, and never seeming to be master of its fortunes. MacDermot's portrait of the gallant little David, boldly and heroically doing battle with the wicked LNWR, is hard to reconcile with the hesitancy and vacillation revealed in the records, yet it was a survivor. It was clearly unfortunate that, unlike the VNR, the NAH had decided to slow progress during the slump. The average time taken to build a railway during the period was 10 miles a year; the TVE took 10 years to cover 15 miles. 150 years later it looks as though the real difference between the two companies was in the quality of their management; management of the strategy and the shareholders by the chairman, and management of the business by the general manager.

Chapter 4

INFRASTRUCTURE

By 1865, the GWR had thus acquired two railways built with the intention of connecting Merthyr to the rest of the world. In reality, although that objective had been attained, the underlying strategy had changed even before the completion of the link at Middle Duffryn, transferring the emphasis to Aberdare. Now, despite the railway being continuous throughout, it remained in many respects two separate lines, one linking the Aberdare valley to Swansea and the other connecting it to Pontypool Road and England: Merthyr seemed to have withdrawn into the mist and rain. The railway comprised sections of single track and mixed gauge, adverse gradients, and an abundance of junctions, curves and speed restrictions, all of which conspired against main line status. Yet in spite of the difficulties of operation, it was to become one of the busiest and most complex lines in the country. This came about because the greater part of its activity was not over its entire length but over sections, its many junctions linking so many lesser and greater routes together. In this respect its role might be compared to that of the M25 motorway.

To a company like the GWR, interested primarily in high speed passenger traffic, this asset was unlikely to receive priority management attention; Joshua Williams' earlier complaint to Potter about the GWR's apparent lack of interest in the coal trade, and the delay in completing the link at Middle Duffryn suggested something less than enthusiasm for the line. All the more remarkable therefore were the tasks it was able to perform, and the weight and density of traffic handled, at its peak, by 64 signal boxes and 20 junctions, all in just 41 miles of railway.

However, whatever its real preferences, the

J. Armstrong's recommendation of the early 1870's, that coal trains should not be formed on the main-line, was clearly being flouted on 21 July 1961, as 2-8-0T No. 5258 emerges from Mountain Ash sidings with part of a coal train. The rest of the train stands on the up main-line. The distant N.C.B. locomotive is No. 11, while 'The Earl' stands alongside 5258.

S. A. Leleux.

GWR was obliged shortly after acquisition to make major improvements. In May 1872 the whole distance of mixed gauge track from Wind Street station in Swansea to Middle Duffryn was converted to standard gauge by removing the third rail. In the previous year the branches in the Dare valley had already been reduced to standard gauge, and a year later Merthyr once again became a one-gauge town. These works coincided with the conversion to standard gauge of the old South Wales main line along the coast.

Other changes were prompted by commercial developments arising in part from the completion of the link between the TVE and the VNR. Growth in coal traffic, especially from Mountain Ash eastward, caused serious congestion. This increased in 1871, and by 1872, 13 coal trains and three long distance goods trains were moved eastward by the GWR from the Aberdare valley each day. In addition, the Rhymney operated 16 trains as far as Penalltau Junction, where they bore south for the docks at Cardiff: by 1885 the total was 40 trains a day. Mounting congestion saw J. Armstrong commissioned by the Board of the GWR to investigate and make recommendations; he found the major delays occurred at Mountain Ash, Quakers Yard and Pontypool Road. The causes were many and various, typified by insufficient sidings, necessitating the shunting and formation of trains on the main line. At Cwmbach for instance, just south of Aberdare, he found that it took one hour for a train to be formed, a process which should have taken 15 minutes; with 150 waggon-loads a day being generated, the trade justified better facilities. On riding a coal train between Mountain Ash and Pontypool Road, Armstrong found that a pick-up goods train had been allowed to depart just before the Birkenhead train on which he was riding; as a consequence his train suffered serious delay. Furthermore the absence of a through telegraph between the former TVE and VNR hardly improved matters. There was also inadequate provision of sidings at Pontypool Road, which had to be approached with caution down the long steep descent, and more generous accommodation was recommended as a result. Armstrong also found that the shunters were trained as guards for emergencies, which meant that, if they were called away, the shunting suffered. To ease the position at Pontypool he recommended the prioritising of through trains and through running to the north without stopping. It was also proving inadequate to supply locomotives for the whole line from Pontypool and a larger running shed was needed at Aberdare.

Armstrong's report carried some weight and seems to have been heeded. The line was doubled from Gelli Tarw through Aberdare to Middle Duffryn by the end of 1872, where it joined the double track from there to Cefn Glas, which had been completed in 1868. The locomotive shed at Aberdare was doubled in size in 1874, and overall capacity was increased in the short term and thereafter progressively at Pontypool Road also.

Further relief to the difficulties caused by the surge in traffic in the early 1870s was obtained in 1873 when the GWR started operating London-bound coal trains down what in 1860 had become the Sirhowy Railway from Tredegar Junction to Newport. The conversion of the SWR to standard gauge made possible a shorter route to London, but this depended upon the co-operation of the Monmouthshire Railway. The opening in 1874 of a direct line from Pontypool to Newport posed a serious threat to the MRCC and led to their leasing the railway to the GWR and selling outright five years later. However, this action by the GWR caused the Sirhowy, upon which the GWR had its eye, to sell out to the LNWR. The GWR thus had a hostile owner between Tredegar Junction and the Monmouthshire at Nine-Mile Point. They therefore looked for another route from the TVE towards Newport and lighted upon Hall's Road. This ran from the TVE west of Crumlin down to the Ebbw valley, joining the Monmouthshire above Nine-Mile Point. The GWR leased this line for 1000 years in 1877, but did not convert it to a railway until 1912. Meanwhile, peace was made with the LNWR, allowing resumption of the use of the Sirhowy route with effect from 1877. This was destined to be the principal route for heavy coal trains bound for the London area and Southampton for as long as the trade lasted.

As locomotives and trains became heavier it was an advantage to have an alternative route to that over the Crumlin Viaduct and down the steep bank to Pontypool. From this time therefore, Pontypool Road dealt mainly in coal-trains for the Midlands and the north of England.

THE LINE DESCRIBED

NEATH AND ITS VALE

The first station at Neath was the SWR station on its main line, slightly south of the site of the present station. Management of this station was a source of trouble for the VNR and in 1859 they obtained Parliamentary approval to acquire a half share in it; this was not however taken up, partly because of the expense, but also because the later construction of the Swansea and Neath rendered Neath station less critical to the VNR's well being. When the SNR opened in 1863, Neath acquired two new stations, Neath Abbey and Neath Low Level, the latter being located just south of the SWR main line where it crossed the SNR. *The Cambrian* newspaper described this station in glowing terms, '. . . Constructed with

red and blue brick with forest stone dressing. The line being in a cutting, the booking offices are on a higher level, and the platforms approached by steps. A covered bridge has been provided for passengers to cross the line and is so arranged that they can only get to and from the up or down platform according to the train by which they may be going or arriving.' (*sic*) When the GWR became the operators of both stations in 1865, they decided to move their main line station to a position close to the Low Level station to facilitate interchange. Two new wooden platforms on the main line were linked to the lower station by stairs and a covered way. However the railway company had not considered the good people of Neath, who campaigned for a return to the *status quo*, complaining that the new joint station was too far out of town.

A combination of public opinion and damage caused by a severe storm in 1869 caused a review of the situation at Neath and in 1872, as part of the planning for the narrowing of the gauge on the old SWR main line, consideration was given to abandoning High Level and re-opening the old station. It was noted that, if High

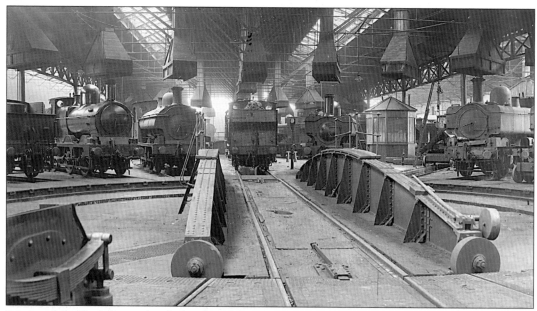

Interior of the Neath locomotive shed at Cwrt Sart on the 9 June 1926. Of the dozen or so locomotives in the picture, only two can be identified with any certainty; Dean Goods 0-6-0 No. 2350 is on the left of the picture and little 0-6-0PT No. 2085 may be seen between two other locomotives in the centre.

WIMM: GW Coll.

Plan of the short-lived attempt by the GWR to combine the main station on the South Wales line with that on the SNR, which eventually became Riverside.
Neath Antiquarian Society.

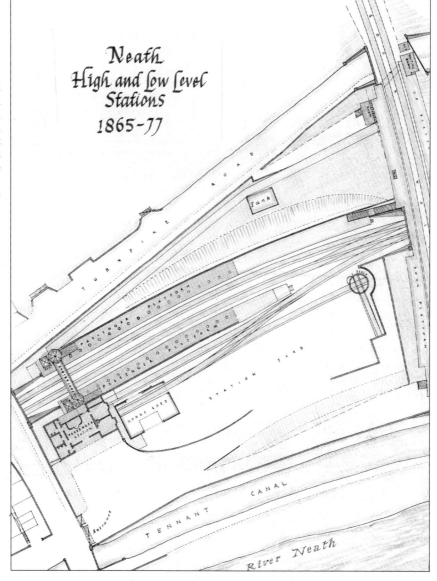

Neath High and Low Level Stations 1865-77

Level was to be retained, it would be necessary to build a permanent structure, together with a cross-over and a siding for carriages. Instead, in 1877, a new station termed Neath General was opened on the main line, just north of the original and on the site of the present station. It was even closer to the town centre than the previous station near this site and was a characteristic GWR structure of the time.

In Swansea, the SNR built a temporary station on the viaduct as their terminus at Wind Street. *The Cambrian* reported, 'One of the arches of the viaduct forms a very large and commodious booking office and the second arch two very comfortable waiting rooms. The arches are lined with galvanised iron and they are so metamorphosed that none but those who know can tell what they were. The platform, which is of wood, built onto the viaduct, is 260 ft long, 16 ft wide, and is approached from the booking office by a bold flight of steps.' From old maps it is possible to conclude that these arches were immediately south of Wind Street and that the island platform may have extended partly over

Neath Riverside Station looking south-west, before removal of awnings, covered way across the tracks, and 'Oriental-looking' turrets. No date.

NMRW.

Neath Riverside Station facing north-east, showing the high level South Wales main-line. No date.

R. H. Marrows Coll.

Neath Riverside Station forecourt. September 1951.

H. C. Casserley, courtesy R. H. Marrows.

0-6-2T No. 5633 approaches Neath General Station with a train from Pontypool Road. No date.
John Davies.

0-6-0PT heading north from Neath Riverside, with the Bridge carrying the South Wales main-line prominent in the background. June 1964.
John Davies.

the street on the railway bridge, although the width, given the need to accommodate two broad gauge tracks also, is questionable. This station had a short life; in 1865, a serious accident occurred at the draw-bridge over the North Dock when a coal train was driven forward across the open bridge. Reluctance thereafter to run passenger trains over this harbour bridge and congestion with coal traffic caused the GWR to switch passenger trains from the Vale of Neath line to Swansea High Street, which meant that, from 1873, the old SNR line became used only by goods trains, and all passenger trains used the former SWR main line. Local services reopened on the SNR line on 1 October 1881, and until 1936 terminated at a new station rather inconveniently located at East Dock. This consisted of an island platform and a modest single-storey station building constructed of wood. When it was

opened, considerable local pressure was brought on the GWR to re-open a station near Wind Street, but this was resisted in deference to the wishes of the coal shippers. By now, too, the LNWR had opened Victoria station, near Wind Street, in the commercial centre of the town; this was being promoted as the most conveniently placed station for London. From 1936, the SNR line to East Dock was closed and Neath Low Level, which had been renamed Riverside in 1926 (having for two years been called Bridge Street), became a terminus for the occasional railcar service to Glyn Neath and for trains on the Neath and Brecon line. Through trains from the Vale of Neath line had to reverse at Neath in order to continue to Swansea where they reverted to the use of High Street station. The station interchange problems in Neath were finally resolved by the closure of the lines to Pontypool and to Brecon.

The first few miles up the Vale of Neath are fairly level in the open part of the valley. The stations at Aberdulais, Resolven and Glyn Neath were undistinguished, although the latter had extensive coal sidings and a branch to the Abernant works, opened in 1879. In 1891 another branch was installed just north of the station, crossing the river and serving Aberpergwm colliery. Banking engines for assisting goods trains up the Glyn Neath bank were housed in the single road engine shed at Glyn Neath.

In addition to the stations, from time to time small halts were built to serve a colliery or works. One of the smallest was Melincourt (sic) Halt, a short wooden platform. Clyne Halt was opened in 1905 to serve the Resolven Tinplate works, whilst north of Glyn Neath, Cwmrhyd-y-Gau Halt served the Abernant brick and tile works from 1935 to 1945. British Rhondda Halt, which had a platform on the down line only, served a colliery of the same name from 1906 to

1911; trains from Swansea terminating there reversed by way of a cross-over just to the north of the platform. In 1911 it was replaced by the two-platform Pontwalby Halt a few yards to the north and beyond the Pontwalby viaduct.

At the top of the Glyn Neath bank the line entered the 526 yd long Pencaedrain tunnel, necessitated by a steep-sided shoulder of mountain which blocked the way forward; on emerging on the north side of the tunnel the railway ran on a ledge cut into the side of a narrow and picturesque valley before emerging into the bleak landscape of Hirwaun Common. The summit was reached at Hirwaun Pond, just beyond Rhigos Halt (built in 1911) and named after the nearby colliery and mountain peak. This was the location of the stopping point for down goods trains. Hirwaun Pond Halt, just east of Rhigos, was built in 1941 to serve a new armaments factory on the nearby Hirwaun Industrial Estate.

Neath General Station forecourt. No date.
WIMM: GW Coll.

2-6-2-T No. 4157 draws away from the stock of a Pontypool Road to Swansea train at Neath General. 26 May 1964.
GBJ.

BR standard 2-6-4-T No. 80133, a regular Vale of Neath line locomotive, having taken over the arrival from Pontypool Road, crosses over onto the down main-line, en route for Swansea. 26 May 1964.

GBJ.

A contemporary engraving of the accident which occurred on 29 September 1865, when broad-gauge locomotive No. 16 of the VNR led its train into the dock through an open drawbridge. Both engine-men were drowned.

ILN, courtesy GBJ.

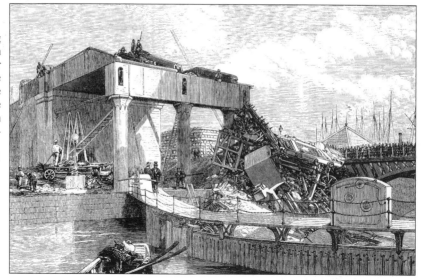

Swansea East Dock Station in September 1951.

NMRW.

Looking east from East Dock Station (in left foreground). August 1967.

R. H. Marrows.

Resolven Station ca. 1905 looking north.

R. H. Marrows Coll.

Resolven Station looking south. June 1963.   R. H. Marrows.

In Resolven, the Clydach Brook and adjacent road cross the VNR at the point indicated by the pedestrian. October 1993.

GBJ.

Threatening storm clouds add drama to this view of Clyne Halt looking north. June 1963.

J. Stone.

The view southward with Clyne Halt in its original condition. September 1926.

WIMM: GW Coll.

Approach to east portal of Pencaedrain Tunnel by BR standard 2-6-4T No. 80133 and Neath-bound train. June 1963.

R. H. Marrows.

Rhigos Halt, looking west, with GW 'pagoda' passenger shelters.

R. W. Kidner Coll.

0-6-0PT No. 3699 with the 3.00 p.m. Swansea to Pontypool Road train near Rhigos. 21 July 1962.

G. T. Robinson.

A rare view of the Rhigos carriage sidings.
R. H. Marrows.

Rhigos halt with Aberdare-bound train.
May 1961.

NMRW.

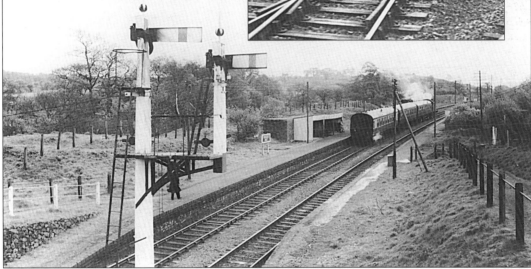

ABERDARE AND ITS VALLEY

Entry into the Cynon valley was across an open stretch of moorland which was ravaged by industry and mineral extraction during the life of the railway and transformed into a forbidding, desolate landscape. Hirwaun (meaning Long Heath) station, a mile from the summit, was built with double track from the outset. This spelling of the name was adopted in 1928 to replace the Anglicised 'Hirwain'. From the opening of the main line to Merthyr in 1853, it became necessary to change trains for Aberdare here, but with the completion of the Middle Duffryn link in 1864, the situation was reversed as Aberdare

once again attained main line status. Thereafter most trains from Merthyr terminated at Hirwaun. Among a number of quarry and industrial lines around Hirwaun, a waggon works of the Gloucester Carriage and Waggon Company was in operation in the early part of this century, close to the site of the Hirwaun Iron Works to the south of the station.

At Gelli Tarw, the single line branch to Merthyr ran straight ahead along the side of the Cynon valley which at this point, within the context of south Wales, is broad and open. The main line to Aberdare, double track from 1872, bore slightly right and noticeably downhill, but

0-6-0PT No. 4688 leaves Hirwaun with a Pontypool Road train. November 1963.

John Davies.

2-6-2T No. 4157 takes water at Hirwaun, prior to departing for Pontypool Road. November 1963.

John Davies.

immediately before this junction the Dare valley branch turned away more acutely and also to the right to cross the Gamlyn viaduct. Sidings at Gelli Tarw were used to assemble coal trains from the Merthyr and Dare branches. The main line down to Aberdare was almost straight though with a gradient of about 1 in 50 for 2 miles.

The 3.55 p.m. train from Pontypool Road to Swansea leaves Hirwaun behind 0-6-2T No. 6641 on 21 August 1962.

G. T. Robinson.

Gelli Tarw junction looking west; 2-6-2T No. 4121 bears away from the straight alignment of the Merthyr line, making for Aberdare. 13 June 1964.

J. Stone.

Trecynon Halt, looking westward up the valley. 11 April 1964.
J. Stone.

Trecynon halt looking east, down the valley. 13 June 1964.
J. Stone.

A mile west of Aberdare, Trecynon Halt was built in 1911. This and the 2 halts east of Aberdare were served by a rail motor service from Swansea East Dock to Mountain Ash. There was also an isolated rail motor service in the Dare and Aman valleys to Cwmaman colliery. This started in 1903 as a workmen's service from a halt called Black Lion Crossing, after the nearby pub, and was extended to become a public service from 1906, with the addition of three small intermediate halts.

When the VNR's approach to the Taff Vale over sharing their station at Aberdare was rebuffed in 1850, the VNR proceeded to build their own. The plan on page 41, drawn for submission to Parliament at the time of the extension to the canal head in 1852, serves to show the layout. The train shed, which survived until the early 1990s, was a wooden building supported on cast iron columns. Here the last train of the day was housed overnight, until a small engine shed shown on the plan was built nearby, just south of the station on what was later (1864) to become the main line. At this time a second engine shed was built, notable for being mixed gauge with four lines.

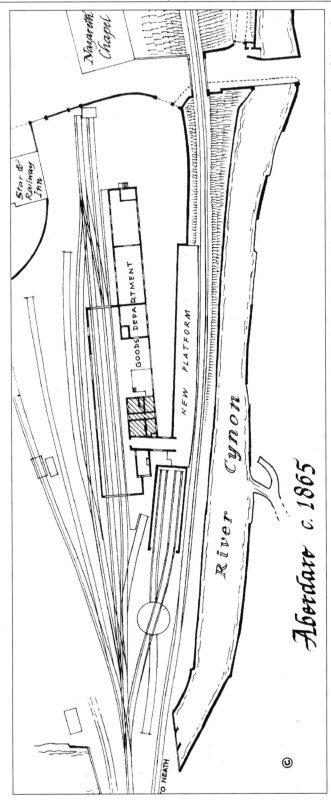

Aberdare c. 1865

Aberdare between 1864 and 1872, showing the first through station prior to the removal of the third rail, the doubling of the track, and the re-location of the engine shed. The shaded area indicates the Booking Office and passenger areas.

GBJ, based on Sandford Survey in Aberdare Library.

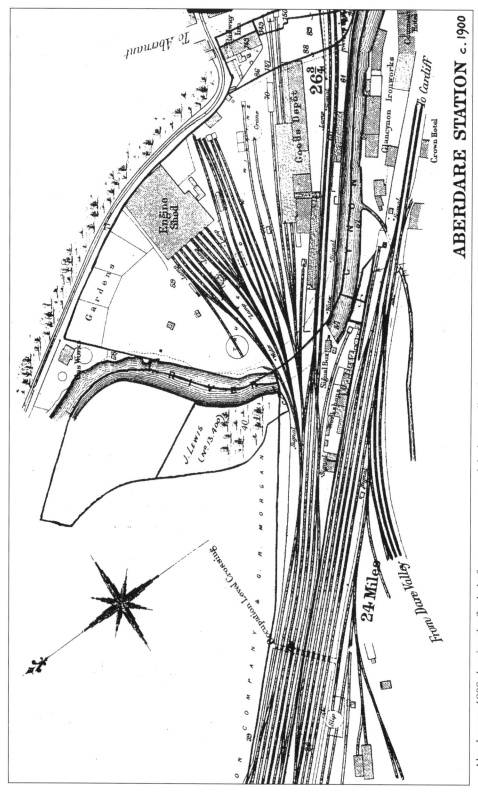

Aberdare ca. 1900 showing the final platform arrangement and the intermediate layout of the engine shed. The TVR lines occupy the lower part of the plan.

PRO

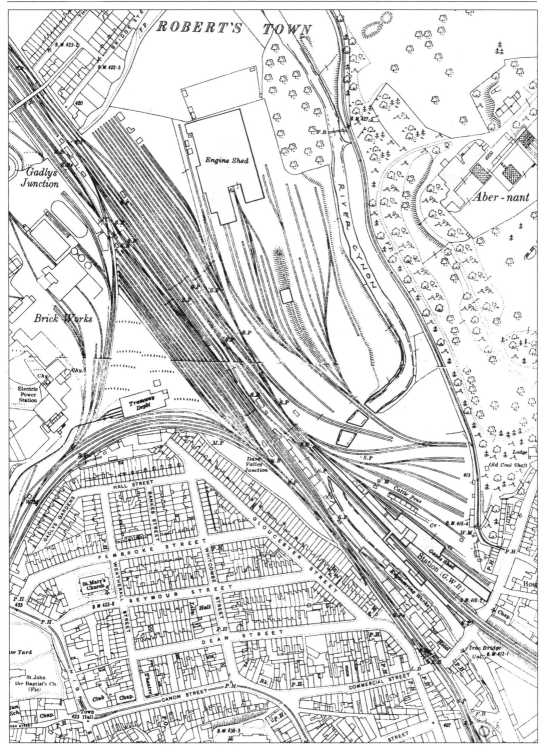

Aberdare in 1920 showing the later engine shed layout. The TVR lines and sidings, as yet without a direct link to the GWR, occupy the lower part of the plan. The Gadlys crossing, scene of an earlier collision, can be seen north-east of the Brick Works, top left of the plan.

O.S. Edition of 1920.

Early in 1864, in preparation for operating trains through Middle Duffryn, a single platform was built, just to the south of the original station, and on the north side of the line. When the third rail was removed and the line doubled in 1872, the original terminus became the goods shed. The provision of a down platform alongside the new track presented a problem as the space between the new alignment and the river Cynon was tight. To accommodate an additional platform, the track was slewed slightly northward, necessitating moving the 1864 platform. The new up platform contained a booking hall and offices which were re-built sometime after 1872 and sympathetically restored in 1995, whilst the old offices survived adjacent to them until the 1970s. Because of site restrictions, the down platform (the only platform in use in the 1990s), had to be staggered east of the up platform, and part of the waiting room was suspended on girders over the river.

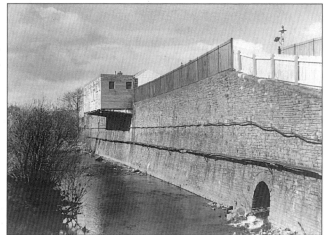

Aberdare Station down platform waiting-room, cantilevered over the River Cynon. ca. 1967.

Glyn Davies.

Aberdare High Level looking west in June 1963.

R. H. Marrows.

A general view of Aberdare Station, facing east, taken probably in the early 1890's and showing the station as built after the removal of the third rail and doubling of the track in 1872.

WIMM: GW Coll.

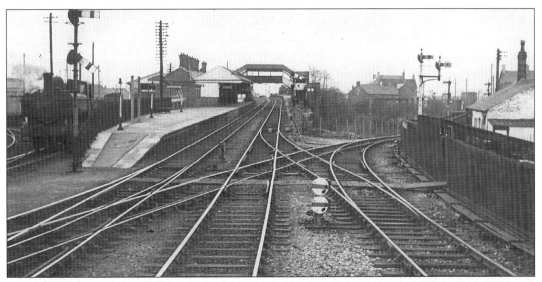

A similar viewpoint to that above, but taken in 1964, reveals some changes to the up side station building and canopy made around the turn of the century, and the link line from the former TVR installed in 1927.

R. H. Marrows.

The first engine shed, which stood south west of the original station, was demolished during the 1872 alterations. As early as 1867, a standard gauge four-road shed had been built in the yard north of the old station, but even this proved insufficient for the increasing traffic and, following Armstrong's report, it was doubled to eight roads. In 1907 a completely new complex was erected, slightly to the west, to accommodate the much longer 2-6-0 and 2-8-0 locomotives then being introduced; the old shed was demolished and replaced with sidings. In 1927, with the closure of the former TVR shed, access was made from the Taff Vale to the Great Western sheds and sidings, just west of the station, by a diagonal crossing on the level; from 1924 this station was called High Level to distinguish it from the former Taff Vale station, which became Low Level.

The difficulty of squeezing two platforms alongside the Cynon River was aggravated by the need to cross a road, which caused the noticeable 'hump' in the line at the eastern end of the station. 2-6-2T No. 4157 has just breasted this 'hump' with a Neath-bound train on 26 May 1964.

GBJ.

Locomotives and staff at Aberdare Shed at the end of the 1890's.

WIMM.

The GWR official photograph of the newly constructed shed and facilities, built to the west of the original in 1908.
WIMM: GW Coll.

Aberdare Shed plan.
WIMM: GW Coll.

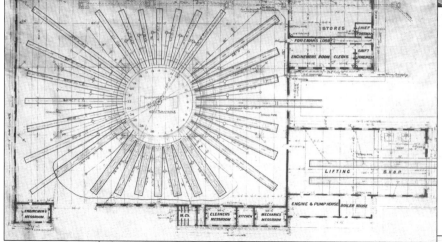

The shed shown above had altered little by the time the line closed. 1964.
H. Frank Evans.

Aberdare Shed Interior, with covered turntable well. May 1951.

H. C. Casserley.

Aberdare Shed Interior, showing planking removed. July 1958.

H. C. Casserley.

This view, looking west from the 'hump' shown on page 118, shows Brunel's original covered station on the right of the picture, later used as a goods ware-house. 6 June 1963.

J. Stone.

The down platform building at Aberdare, which resembled that at Riverside in Neath, gives the appearance of having suffered little alteration since construction in 1872, though the appendage received some minor modifications by 1967, as seen on page 116. The distant backing signal is noteworthy. 6 May 1951.

H. C. Casserley.

There were two halts at various times below Aberdare. The first, at Cwmbach, was just west of a crossing of the line on the level by the TVR which gave access to Lletty Shenkin colliery. The people of Cwmbach had been campaigning for a station for some 36 years when in 1899 the GWR decided to concede, the local colliery owner Powell Duffryn having offered to pay 2/6d. per man per month, with a minimum of £30 per month, for a train to be operated from Aberdare to Cwmbach crossing. Despite this, nothing was done, presumably because the GWR expected the local authority to build the footbridge and agreement could not be reached. Eventually, in 1914, with rising competition from the recently opened tramway system, two platforms and a footbridge were erected. About a mile and a half down the line another halt was built at Duffryn Crossing, also in 1914. As a wartime measure it was closed in 1917 and never reopened.

Cwmbach Halt, looking down the valley. 11 April 1964.

J. Stone.

Hawksworth pannier tank No. 8495, approaching Cwmbach Halt from the east, passes Lletty Shenkin Signal Box. 8 July 1959.

F. K. Davies.

Further down the valley at Mountain Ash, the West MR built a station, completed in 1864, on the north side of the then single line. The link to the TVR was put in shortly afterwards by means of a bridge crossing the nearby Cynon at an acute angle, just west of the West MR station. When the main line was doubled in 1868 a down platform was built on the south side as an island platform with a south face onto the TVR link line. Both platforms were lengthened in 1899, and in 1904 the station entrance was built, together with a verandah covering part of the up platform. At the same time the down platform was widened and provided with a waiting room, and a new footbridge was built between the platforms. From 1924 this station was suffixed Cardiff Rd. to distinguish it from the former TVR station, which became Oxford Street.

The only other station built below Aberdare was in 1899, opposite Penrhiwceiber, where the line crossed over the Aberdare Canal. It was located on an embankment and across the river from the bulk of the population at this part of the valley, who were already well served by the TVR station. Penrhiwceiber High Level, as it was called from 1924, was a simple affair with wooden platforms, small wooden passenger shelters, and no sidings or other facilities. The platforms were linked by a passage-way under the lines, and access to the station from the village was up a long slope on the down side. There was also an entrance from the main road on the up side. Until road works in 1993, the site was readily discernible in its remarkably rural setting.

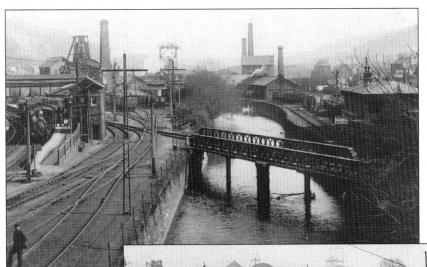

This is thought to be the only photograph of the line at Mountain Ash linking the TVE (on the left) with the TVR (on the right). In the GWR station a 2-4-0 Metro tank waits with an Aberdare-bound train. In the background is Nixon's Colliery. No date.

WIMM.

By June 1963 the scene portrayed above had changed little, except for the removal of the link line across the River Cynon.

R. H. Marrows.

From the down platform at Mountain Ash, looking down the valley, it was possible to discern the location of Cresselley Crossing in the distance. Flooding was often a problem at this point. 6 June 1963.
R. H. Marrows.

The Cresselley crossing and foot-bridge, much used by photographers. June 1963.
R. H. Marrows.

The 11.00 a.m. Aberdare to Pontypool Road train, hauled by 0-6-2T No. 6690, passes Cresselley Crossing Signal Box on 13 March 1964.
G. T. Robinson.

On the up side of the track at Penrhiwceiber High Level there was wild mountain scenery, while on the other side of the line and across the valley, lay the massed housing of a teeming industrial complex. April 1955.

H.C. Casserley.

The setting of Penrhiwcwiber High Level on the edge of the crowded valley; the Aberdare Canal, the remotely located booking office, and the distant TVR station are all discernible. Ca. 1905.

R.H. Marrows Coll.

Penrhiwceiber High Level looking west. June 1963.

R. H. Marrows.

Penrhiwceiber High Level looking east. April 1964.

R.H. Marrows.

FROM THE CYNON TO THE TAFF AND THE RHYMNEY

Between the Cynon and Taff valleys lies a high, steep-sided ridge of mountain, and access between the two valleys was by the 703 yd. long Cefn Glas tunnel, built between 1858 and 1864. Completion was intended in 1861 but was delayed for reasons unrecorded. It is not clear whether these delays contributed to the procrastination over the completion of the rail link at Middle Duffryn, or whether, as seems more likely, they were a consequence. Although the rest of the Aberdare extension from Quakers Yard was laid out to accommodate double track, the tunnel was single from the outset; and so it remained. The line through the bore rises at 1 in 100 in an eastward direction, against loaded mineral trains, and being narrow, unventilated, and damp, was a constant challenge to train crews. An easterly wind would cause the crew of any banking engine to hope that the train engine had shut off steam, otherwise they were likely to be short of air in the narrow tunnel. The situation became even worse in 1904 when the tunnel was re-lined. With barely a hand's clearance from the side of the cab in places, footplate staff were often compelled to seek air on the floor of the cab. Another hazard was presented in winter by icicles, which would form on Sundays in cold weather, when there were very few trains; they were hard to see in the dark, early on Monday mornings.

From the eastern mouth of the tunnel the train emerged via a short cutting in the side of the mountain to enter the Taff valley at a particularly interesting location, where roads, railways, river and canal all carved their respective paths through difficult hilly terrain. Here the river Taff abandons its normal southerly direction to flow in an expansive eastward loop, in a deep gorge through an outcrop of Pennant Sandstone. On the eastern side of the loop was a Society of Friends graveyard; the adjacent village was appropriately called Quakers Yard. Passengers emerging from Cefn Glas tunnel would have passed just beneath the Glamorganshire Canal immediately before they broke into daylight. On leaving the cutting their train crossed the river Taff on a seven arch, 130 yd long masonry viaduct (1864), the final

opening of which carried the railway over the route of the famous Penydarren Tramroad. The TVR main line, crossed by a plate girder bridge, was the last obstacle before the junction with the GW/RR joint Merthyr branch which trailed in on the northern side, just short of Quakers Yard High Level station. This line also crossed the Taff on a masonry viaduct which, like its neighbour and that nearby on the Taff Vale main line, suffered continually from subsidence and had to be shored up with timber.

In 1858 when the TVE was opened to join the Taff at Quakers Yard, the TVR built a nicely proportioned but modest stone station at the junction. Predictably called Quakers Yard Junction it was operated by the NAH, with shared costs. When the extension to Aberdare was completed in 1864, the Great Western, who by then owned the line, built a new station (High Level) adjacent to but above the older station, which had its name changed from Quakers Yard Junction to Quakers Yard Low Level. High Level was an unpretentious affair built mainly of timber; the two stations were linked by a long footbridge and stairs. This interchange became less important in 1886 when the GWR/RR joint line from High Level to Merthyr, up the west side of the Taff, was opened. In 1951, the situation reverted to the original as the joint line was closed when its viaduct over the Taff became unsafe. However, passengers were never the most important feature of this railway complex; it was primarily a double junction and marshalling location for freight trains. East of the stations, the old TVE and the Aberdare extension joined at Quakers Yard East and interchange sidings were provided. Here, during the first half of the century, countless coal trains from the Merthyr area were assembled for movement to England or to Cardiff docks over the Rhymney. Congestion at this location during the First World War was such that, in order to by-pass it, coal from the Rhondda was taken to the Rhymney Railway and introduced by way of Pontypridd and Aber Junction to the Vale of Neath line at Hengoed on its way to the north of England.

Beyond Quakers Yard the railway wound its way round the side of the hill overlooking the

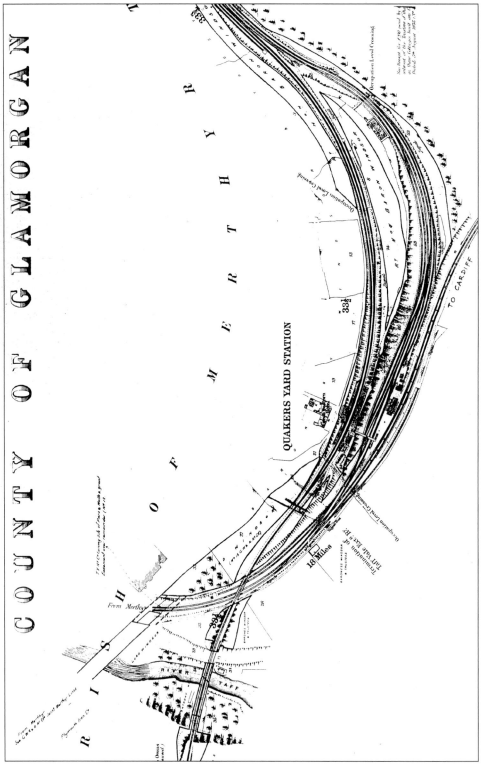

Map of Quakers Yard ca. 1884. The outline plan for the GW/RR Joint Line to Merthyr is shown upper left. The Great Western Hotel survives.   PRO.

dramatic loop in the Taff. One mile to the east, Treharris station was opened in 1880, with the ticket office at road level on the north or town side due to the narrow confines of the cutting; on the south side was the Royal Hotel. The station was placed on such a tight curve that passenger trains were not allowed to pass there.

The approach to Cefn Glas Tunnel with 2-8-0T No. 5249 and an unusual train consisting of 3 coal waggons and 10 brake-vans. No date.

W. E. Spurrier, courtesy S. G. Whittaker.

Looking up the Taff Valley with Quakers Yard to the right, the first viaduct carried the TVE, the second the GW/RR Joint. Both suffered from subsidence, necessitating the timber supports. March 1958.

S. Rickard.

Set against an impressive back-drop of mountain and coal-tip 0-6-2T No. 6605 heads the 4.20 p.m. Neath to Hengoed High Level into Quakers Yard. 20 April 1962.
                    G. T. Robinson.

An engineman's view of the token-less single line section, leading into the Cefn Glas Tunnel. The GW/RR Joint line which led off to the right was closed in 1951 due to subsidence. June 1963.
                    R. H. Marrows.

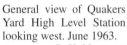

General view of Quakers Yard High Level Station looking west. June 1963.
                    R. H. Marrows.

East-bound passenger train entering Quakers Yard High Level with 0-6-2T No. 6628. August 1963.

J. R. P. Hunt.

Quakers Yard Low Level Station showing the TVE emerging on the left and descending to join the former TVR main-line. 13 June 1964. *W. Potter, courtesy S. G. Whittaker.*

Quakers Yard East Junction Signal Box looking towards Treharris. The actual junction lay behind the photographer. 11 April 1964.

J. Stone.

An unusual con-
figuration descends
from East Junction
towards the Low
Level station. 30
November 1957.
R. M. Casserley.

Metro tank and train
round the curve into
Treharris Station, heading
towards Quakers Yard. No
date.
Lens of Sutton.

Treharris with goods
train. 11 April 1964.
R. H. Marrows.

Treharris looking west, showing road-level booking office. June 1963.
R. H. Marrows.

Treharris Viaduct over the Bargoed Taff River. No date.
D. L. Morgan, courtesy E. A. Evans.

General view of Trelewis with TVE curving away to the right and the entrance to Ocean Deep Navigation Colliery on the left. Early twentieth century.

R.H. Marrows Coll.

Immediately beyond Treharris were junctions with Ocean Deep Navigation colliery, opened in 1879, and with Taff Merthyr colliery, opened in 1924. Between them the railway crossed the Treharris viaduct which was built over the Bargoed Taff river where it tumbled down the steep hillside to the Taff below. The spaces between the arches of the viaduct were gradually filled with coal waste until it became completely embedded. Just beyond was Trelewis Halt, a sparse affair with small wooden shelters. This was not to be confused with another halt a quarter of a mile away on the GW/RR joint line to Dowlais called Trelewis Platform, which was even more threadbare than its neighbour, with platforms made originally from old sleepers and ballast; both were installed in an attempt to compete with buses.

A mere half-mile further on, the scene changes and broadens out at Nelson & Llancaiach. Above the railway to the north stands Llancaiach Fawr, a fine sixteenth century Manor house which has managed to survive the tide of coal mining which at one time threatened to engulf it. The NAH built a station nearby

called Llancaiach. Liddell designed a simple stone building which stood on the south platform, and an island platform without buildings or bridge was built later to the north. By 1912, this station had become congested, as nearby Nelson had developed as a market town with a cattle auction; a reminder that throughout the most intense coal mining activity, parts of industrial south Wales retained their agricultural connections. The GWR accordingly built a brand new station slightly west of the original and west also of the junction with the TVR Nelson branch. This connection was made sometime before 1882 and was generally little used; the branch closed in 1932. The new station was called Nelson & Llancaiach and was to standard GWR specification of the time. The down platform on the south side housed the ticket office and main entrance from Nelson, whilst the north face of the island platform served those trains from the Dowlais branch which terminated there; the south face served trains for Pontypool Road and for Cardiff by way of Ystrad Mynach. East of the station, on the north side, extensive sidings served Werncaiach colliery in the 1920s.

Ocean and Taff Merthyr Collieries from a position near Trelewis Halt. April 1964.
R. H. Marrows.

A well loaded coal train approaches Trelewis Halt on the up line, hauled by 0-6-0PT No. 3753. 14 August 1957.
S. Rickard.

A general view of Trelewis Halt, looking west towards the collieries and Treharris. May 1958.

NMRW

The generous provision of space is evident in this view of Nelson and Llancaiach, looking east. No date.

GBJ Coll.

A panoramic view looking east at Nelson and Llancaiach. A Dowlais train stands at the outer face of the island platform. June 1963.

R. H. Marrows.

Empty ballast waggons heading west from Nelson and Llancaiach. 20 August 1962.

G. T. Robinson.

A passenger's view of Nelson and Llancaiach Station from a train bound for Aberdare. May 1964.
Alan Jarvis.

A train waits on the truncated remains of the former TVR branch from Ponty-pridd, as a west-bound passenger train arrives at Nelson and Llancaiach. No date.
Alan Jarvis.

The section from Nelson & Llancaiach to Penalltau junction, a mile away, proved to be the busiest part of the line; around 1913 over 50 trains a day in each direction were scheduled on weekdays. (See Flow Diagram on page 166.) At Penalltau the RR slipped away to the south towards Ystrad Mynach and Cardiff. This important link had been opened in 1871 and, through running powers granted by the GWR all the way up to Hirwaun, provided the Rhymney with a major new source of traffic. The Vale of Neath line continued from Penalltau across a short colliery line called the Cylla branch from Ystrad, and then around the breast of the hill, affording fine views of the Rhymney valley opening up to the south, past a rather grand row of late Victorian villas whose drawing rooms had a magnificent view of the coal sidings; and so to Hengoed.

Penalltau Junction Signal Box, showing the Rhymney line to Ystrad Mynach falling away in the foreground, while the TVE line is behind the box. No date.

WIMM: GW Coll.

Penalltau Junction looking east towards the signal box, showing the RR diverging to the right and dropping sharply downhill. No date.

R. Roper, courtesy E. A. Evans.

FROM THE RHYMNEY TO THE SIRHOWY AND THE EBBW

The stretch of line between the Rhymney and the Sirhowy is through a generally more gentle landscape. At the point of crossing, the Rhymney valley is broad, deep, green, and steep-sided, and presented a significant obstacle to the engineers seeking to minimise the gradients. The Sirhowy, in contrast, is on a much smaller scale; its crossing was therefore comparatively easy.

Where the Rhymney passed under the TVE at Hengoed, the RR had its own station (called Hengoed) which, from the start, was run jointly with the station called Rhymney Junction on the TVE. Transfer of mineral waggons was made west of here. About 1890 the GWR put in a direct southward link, known as the Hengoed loop, between the TVE and the RR which,

among other things, permitted LNWR trains access from the Sirhowy valley to Cardiff. On 1 June 1905 Hengoed station was renamed 'Hengoed & Maesycwmmer', presumably an attempt by the Rhymney to upstage the Brecon & Merthyr, which had a station on the other side of the valley called just 'Maesycwmmer', though for a time, as though to add to the confusion, that was known as 'Maesycwmmer & Hengoed'. From 1 July 1906, however, the GWR followed the Rhymney's example and called its station 'Hengoed & Maesycwmmer'. When they all became part of the GWR in 1923, 'Maesycwmmer' reverted to its original name, whilst the others became 'Hengoed High and Low Level'. Now that only the Low Level station remains, it is again just 'Hengoed'. It stands as a charming survivor.

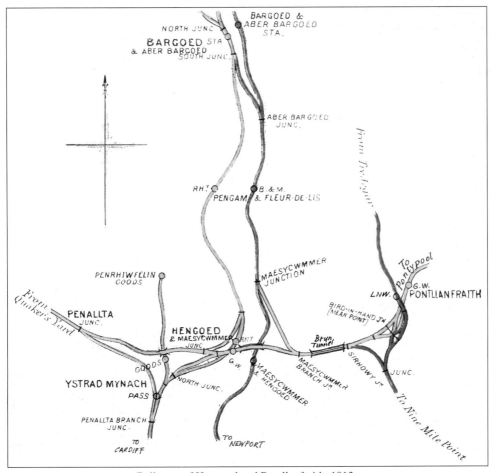

Railways of Hengoed and Pontllanfraith. 1913.

Railway Clearing House.

Hengoed High Level looking west, showing the Hengoed loop diverging to the left. 0-6-2T No. 5633, running bunker first, heads the 1.10 p.m. from Pontypool Road. 13 April 1963.
R. H. Marrows.

Doubtless the inhabitants of the Victorian villas in the background took no notice of the passage of this short east-bound goods train. No date.
R. E. Troop.

Hengoed High Level Station, looking east. April 1964.
R. H. Marrows.

It was still possible to see the two levels east of Penalltau Junction in 1994, with the singled former RR line towards Cardiff still in regular use by coal trains.

DD.

Pub sign at Hengoed illustrating the two levels. No date.

Alan Jarvis.

By 1994, the view from the houses west of Hengoed High Level was decidedly more rural.

DD.

Hengoed High Level occupied an elevated, restricted site, squeezed between the TVE bridge over the Rhymney main line and the Hengoed Viaduct, frequently referred to as the Maesycwmmer Viaduct, and in early references as the Rhymney Viaduct. 298 yds long on 16 stone arches, 130 ft high and on a slight curve, it is still much admired. Started in mid 1853, it was the last major piece of the TVE to be completed before opening in 1858. On the eastern side of the valley, the Brecon & Merthyr main line passed under the viaduct through a special skewed arch; a connection from it trailed in on the up side of the TVE at Maesycwmmer Junction. The NAH had sought authority to build such a link in 1853 (it is marked on the 1853 end-paper map) and the B & M sought to make it in 1860, but the state of the track on the B & M, or Old Rumney tramroad was too poor to allow interchange until 1863.

Smoke and fog combine on a frosty morning to create a picturesque image as 2-6-0 No. 6361 crosses the Hengoed Viaduct with the 7.40 a.m. train from Neath to Pontypool Road. 22 December 1962.

G. T. Robinson.

Early engraving of the Hengoed Viaduct. No date.

WIMM.

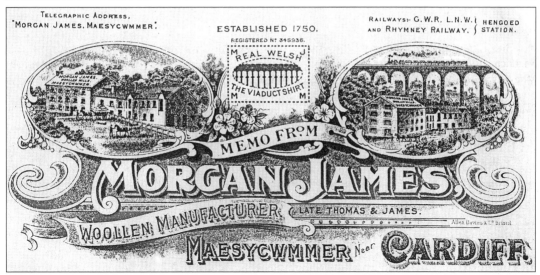

Letterhead of the Woollen Mill located beneath the Hengoed Viaduct, showing an imaginative adoption of the viaduct as a logo.

GBJ Coll.

Shortly after this junction, the line entered a cutting leading to the Bryn Tunnel, 398 yds long and completed in 1857, which took the line through the high ground between the Rhymney and the Sirhowy. On emerging, the line passed through another cutting which gradually opened out at a complex tangle of four junctions known collectively in later years as Bird-in-Hand

Junction, after a nearby pub. Originally this was simply the place where the TVE passed under the Sirhowy Tramway, with some sidings for the interchange of coal waggons. Then in 1873 the link was made from the west to the south to enable GWR coal trains from Aberdare to take a short cut down the Sirhowy valley to the Great Western main line at Newport. About 1890, the

Bird-in-Hand West Box, looking east. June 1963.

R. H. Marrows.

A closer view of Bird-in-Hand West Box, showing the link line bearing right towards the LNWR Sirhowy branch, crossed, almost immediately, by the TVE link to the Sirhowy line. June 1963.

R. H. Marrows.

Pontllanfraith Low Level Station looking east. April 1964.

Alan Jarvis.

0-6-0PT No. 3708 leaving Pontllanfraith Low Level, and heading towards Bird-in-Hand Junction. The row of shops and houses on the right survive as a marker, as all evidence of the railway has gone. April 1964.

Alan Jarvis.

LNWR, who had by then acquired the Sirhowy Railway, made a direct link between their southward line and the TVE to enable their trains to run from the Sirhowy valley to Ystrad Mynach and Cardiff. The complex was completed by the insertion of the link from the TVE down line towards the south which necessitated crossing the LNWR link line on the level. Originally the stations at the junction were called 'Tredegar Junction', and a nearby pub of the same name still bears witness to the fact. Unlike Hengoed, these stations were not jointly run. Eventually, desire for individual identity led the GWR on 1 May 1905 to rename their station 'Pontllanfraith' which, once more, must have caused confusion, because on 1 July 1911 both were re-named, as Pontllanfraith High or Low Level stations. Their appearance revealed their parenthood: High Level had no pretentions other than those of a minor LNWR station—it was merely a cluster of small single storey wooden buildings of rather basic appearance; Low Level, on the other hand, was charmingly romantic, constructed in rough stone with gables, and iron and glass platform awnings, a cheering statement by an impoverished railway. It closely resembled the first station at Pontypool Road, the main building being almost a mirror image of that at the larger station.

Penar Junction looking east, with Hall's Road to the right. June 1963.

R. H. Marrows.

Pentwynmawr Halt looking east. April 1963.

R. H. Marrows.

Crumlin Low Level Station and the Ebbw Valley, seen from a train crossing the viaduct. April 1963.

R. H. Marrows.

0-6-0PT No. 9609 at the western end of the Crumlin Viaduct, with the 7.38 a.m. train from Pontypool Road to Aberdare. 13 June 1964.

G. T. Robinson.

The crossing of the Sirhowy river was on an embankment above the single-arched stone bridge, which as a result had the appearance of being little more than a large culvert.

Around the next bend lay another junction, Penar Junction, at which Hall's Road crossed the TVE diagonally and dropped sharply into a tunnel leading straight down towards the Ebbw valley. This was named after Benjamin Hall, a local landowner, whose son, as Clerk to the Commissioners of Works, gave his name to 'Big Ben'. Here a small halt called Penar Junction Halt was opened in 1913 for a few years and, just beyond the junction, another called Pentwynmawr followed in 1926. A little further on, Treowen Halt was opened in 1927, in

connection with a short-lived service of passenger trains to Oakdale, located up Hall's Road.

The approach to Crumlin was high above the Ebbw valley, around the breast of the hill, and past an unexpectedly Italian-looking campanile on a white church. Crumlin High Level station thus lived up to its name, which it kept unaltered from opening in 1857. It was another solidly built NAH stone station, perched on the side of an extremely steep hill, with an excellent view of the viaduct. Changing trains between the two stations at Crumlin involved a descent of some 200 ft to Low Level station which was down in the valley on the former Monmouthshire Railway (Western Valleys) line from Newport.

2-6-2T No. 4114 on Crumlin Viaduct heading east. No date.

Alan Jarvis.

Crumlin Viaduct with the former MRCC Western Valleys line in the foreground. August 1963.

Alan Jarvis.

THE CRUMLIN VIADUCT

'Beautiful ! You are right. It is beautiful. From east to west, high above the lovely valley, high above the nestling houses and the glittering waters, stretches the lacelike viaduct, light and delicate as if it were the work of the fairy Ariel. It is a work of the brain, pre-eminent above the hands. So slight does it appear, that even now, though it has stood the severest tests, and has been a thing established for thirteen years, many persons are still too timorous to cross it. Of its perfect strength and safety there cannot be the least doubt in the minds of sensible people.' So wrote W.H. Greene in 1870.

By far the greatest single achievement of the NAH was the construction of this viaduct across the Ebbw river at Crumlin. At first sight it may seem surprising that what was then still a minor mineral railway, in a corner of the country away from the main thrust of railway investment, should have been responsible for building what was once one of the highest railway bridges in the world; it was also an early example of the application of the so-called Warren truss wrought iron span. However the world of railway promoters and builders was a close network and all the players in the NAH scene were linked with the fast moving world of civil engineering.

Charles Liddell, who became Engineer to the NAH in 1851, was an established professional and was shortly to take on simultaneously the engineering of part of the Midland Railway extension from Leicester to Hitchin. His partner, Gordon, was the first Professor of Engineering at Glasgow University. Thomas Kennard, the contractor who built the viaduct, was the son of Robert Kennard M.P. who had made a fortune in the first railway boom of the thirties as a banker. With an eye to the future, he had bought the Falkirk Ironworks, which specialised in castings, and the Blaenavon Ironworks—only four miles from Crumlin—which specialised in the production of high quality wrought iron. Kennard's neighbour in Hertfordshire happened to be another M.P. Sir Samuel Peto, the railway contractor, who in partnership with Thomas Brassey constructed parts of the Eastern Counties, South Eastern, and Great Northern

Railways—and, indeed, railways all over the world.

A director of the South Eastern Railway at this time was Daniel Warren whose brother, James Warren—an untrained but clever engineer—invented a number of practical applications of iron such as cast metal screws. In 1848 he patented what became known as the Warren truss which used equilateral triangles. It is estimated that his drawings would have enabled construction of spans of between 60 and 100 ft. They were claimed to be superior to the earlier so-called Neville truss, which used narrow isosceles triangles. The first Warren-truss bridge was built at London Bridge station on the South Eastern Railway in 1850.

In 1851 the Great Northern was faced with the crossing of the Trent at Newark. A freelance consultant Charles Wild had developed a Warren truss span of 250 ft which was adopted by the GNR engineer James Cubitt; he happened to be the son of the engineer of the South Eastern, and the Newark bridge became something of a landmark in engineering history.

The Kennards first became associated with the Warren truss in 1851 when they tendered unsuccessfully for the construction of bridges in India. In that year Robert Kennard was elected an Associate Member of the Institute of Civil Engineers. His seconders were an impressive line-up of railway engineers, including Peto, Stephenson, and the Cubitts, father and son. In 1853 his son Tom took out two patents: one was a modification of the Warren truss; the other covered the use of cast iron pipes clustered in a hexagonal shape to form bridge piers. These were used in the Crumlin Viaduct.

The authorship of the Crumlin Viaduct design is not totally clear. Charles Liddell accepted responsibility for the design and for choosing the Warren truss span, and in 1854 told shareholders that his views on the method of construction, which had led him to advise it to the board and shareholders, had been confirmed by the stability of the first pier. But Tom Kennard was almost certainly designer of the piers, and it was he who submitted the patent application for modifying the Warren truss. Liddell acknowledged that he had received advice from Wild on the truss principle, so it would seem that he was at the very least a supportive client, possibly more; but Tom Kennard's patent application demonstrates that, unlike Wild, he was aware of the need to construct the diagonals in such a way that a moving load of great weight could be supported. Mr Keith Horne of Ross-on Wye has pointed out that this was probably the first time in Britain that this was acknowledged, and steps taken to cope with it; this probably accounts for the fact that the viaduct was able to survive so long, bearing continually increasing loads. It was, in any case, Tom Kennard who submitted the project to the NAH board in July 1852. The meeting was held, as was often the case, in the London Tavern in Bishopsgate and in August it was decided to invite tenders for a wrought iron bridge 'over five openings of 200ft wide.' In September, Carr, the resident engineer, was instructed to supply plans and the specification for the ground works to the Kennards, who were to be free to alter the spans in the interests of cost, safety and strength. On 1 October, Liddell reported in favour of Kennard's 'Warren bridge' over the so called lattice bridge proposed by the other bidder, Doyne. This was accepted. It would seem that Liddell, having decided on an iron girder bridge on the grounds of cost, had already chosen who was going to build the viaduct and to what design. Doyne, who had previously designed a bridge over the Taff at Treforest, was not a serious contender. The agreement with the Kennards was confirmed on 20 October.

In the event, the bridge consisted of ten 150 ft spans in groups of seven and three, separated by a hill, and over 200 ft above the valley floor. Although always treated as one structure it was thus, in fact, two.

The Kennards had the wrought iron, the cast iron and the technology for the spans and the piers. All they needed was an assembly plant. In 1853 the Crumlin Viaduct Works was completed, with rail connection to the MRCC just north of the line of the viaduct. Its role was primarily to supply parts for the building of the viaduct, but it eventually supplied fabricated parts to India and countries in Europe as well. In December of the same year the first cast iron pier was lifted into place; this was marked with a ceremony and it

was reported that the NAH chairman's wife, Lady Isabella Fitzmaurice, buried contemporary coins in an inscribed cup in the base; one year later in December 1854 the first truss was lifted into position. In April 1855 there was a serious accident when one of the girders linking the brick abutment to the first iron pier slipped as it was being lifted into place and fell, dragging its three fellows with it; two men were killed. Nevertheless the seven span section was complete by August 1855 and the smaller three span section by that December. But the whole structure remained unopened for another year and a half.

When the contract was let in October 1852, it had been stipulated that completion should be by 1 October 1854. It is not clear what caused the near three year delay, but it is possible that it took longer than expected to raise the first piers, due to the need to build masonary foundations for the central pair, and to drain and clear part of the canal to do so. This may account for the somewhat premature celebrations with Lady Isabella, which could have been a device intended to impress shareholders with the magnitude of the task so far achieved. The delay certainly coincided with the declining interest the LNWR was taking in the NAH. A further delay may have occurred following the accident

Pier of the Crumlin Viaduct at ground level. No date.
NMRW.

Repair work on the Crumlin Viaduct, looking east towards Crumlin Junction. No date.

WIMM: GW Coll.

referred to above, but by then the original deadline had in any case been exceeded.

In August 1854 shareholders were told that work had been slow for the previous six months, but that it should be complete by May 1855 in time for the opening of the line from Pontypool to Crumlin. In March 1855 contractors were told that work on the viaduct and the Bryn tunnel was to be kept within an expenditure level of £1,000 per month. The final delay of eighteen months from the end of 1855, by which time it was nearly complete, was blamed in a report to the board of November 1856 on exceptionally wet weather. Almost certainly, more lay behind the subsidiary comment that in any case there was no point in opening the viaduct until the railway could be opened as far as the Sirhowy Tramroad. This had been deliberately delayed by the financial constraint which had to be exercised at that time. In February 1856 shareholders were told that work on the Sirhowy junction and other links had been stopped, but by August they were being told that the suspension of work between Crumlin and the Sirhowy had been lifted. Kennard himself said he could have completed the work in half the 3½ years it took from erecting the first pier. This claim is born out by his work elsewhere; a bridge over the Ebro 2,100

ft long took only eight months; a bridge similar to Crumlin near Rome took only a month. The Belah viaduct, a similar but smaller structure in Westmorland, took only four months.

By May 1857, the viaduct was ready for testing. In the presence of Professor Gordon, Liddell, M.W. Carr the resident engineer, T.W. and H.M. Kennard and others, six locomotives and waggons each loaded with lead and weighing 380 tons in all, were run onto one of the spans, using both lines of track. The maximum deflection observable was between 1 inch and 1¼ inch. When the full weight was in place, Carr startled all present by climbing over the rails of the bridge, clinging to the iron work, and minutely examining the works to check whether there was any giving way. A few days later Colonel Wynne, the Inspector, passed the viaduct as safe and expressed his unqualified admiration. It was opened with great celebrations on Whit Monday, 1 June. Excursion trains brought people from many parts of the country and a crowd of 20,000 was estimated to be present. Locomotives on the line and the Western Valleys line below were decorated with ribbons, flags, and evergreens. An arch of evergreens and flowers over the centre of the viaduct bore banners inscribed, 'Long life and prosperity to

T.W. Kennard'. Two cannon fired volleys all day, causing the mountains 'to reverberate with their thunder', according to the local press.

Two hundred of the more distinguished people present were entertained to lunch at T.W. Kennard's nearby residence, Crumlin Hall. Two hundred of the workers were also entertained a few days later. After the lunch the Hon. William Fitzmaurice made what appears to have been an appropriately happy and diplomatic speech, praising the engineers and contractors and making special mention of his Deputy Chairman, Robinson, and of fellow directors Brown and Jones. In an insight into his own character he said that as a younger son, he had always endeavoured to advance in proportion to the difficulties he encountered. Rennie in his speech referred to the importance, to the fortunes of the NAH, of the £40,000 invested in the company by Mr Brown, without which he doubted whether the company could have survived. He ended by expressing the hope that all engineers would be activated by the same honest spirit as Mr Liddell.

Then, almost as soon as the party was over, problems began to emerge. Already in July attention was being drawn to items in the Kennard account which had not been agreed. By February 1858 negotiations had reached the point where Kennard had offered to settle for £50,000, but the board of the NAH were holding out for £46,000. Liddell had revised his assessment of cost upward from the original £40,000 to £42,000 and in addition there were costs for rails and switches. In the absence of progress, in July 1859, the Kennards issued a writ for payment; the NAH accountants paid £944 into court, representing their best assessment of what was payable after netting transport costs against the costs of rails. The difference between the NAH figure and the £62,000 generally quoted as the arbitrator's final assessment is not explained. It is possible that it included work on the foundations not carried out by Kennards, but the most likely explanation lies in the extra costs in wages alone, incurred as a result of the NAH holding back construction. Henry Maynard in his Handbook on the Crumlin Viaduct simply refers to higher costs incurred by the Kennards. It was probably impossible to lay off the workers completely, as,

no doubt, the NAH kept changing their position, as their view of the funds flow position fluctuated, and the wages of 200 men at say £50 for a year could explain much of the discrepancy.

Meanwhile the viaduct was not without its technical problems. In the hot summer of 1859, metal expansion led to a lateral movement of the track. Towards the end of the year, when Liddell was inconveniently abroad, the down line had to be temporarily closed while adjustments were made to the girders under the up line. Martin Kennard was banned from access. However by the end of January 1860, Liddell had returned, had approved the alterations to the up line, and having run three locomotives over it, had pronounced it safe. Kennard was reinstated and the same work was done on the down line.

Trouble re-occurred in 1865. Again it stemmed from lateral movement. This time the public became aware that something was wrong and a Government Inspector was called. In order to improve the rigidity, the wooden deck was replaced with wrought iron transverse girders. On these were laid longitudinal girders upon which the rails rested. Finally the whole was floored with wrought iron sheet, and the two tracks were moved closer together to bring the weight of trains closer to the centre.

Ten years later the bridge was tested again and found to be secure. And so it lasted until 1928. Locomotives now some five times the weight they were when the structure was designed, and immensely heavy traffic during the First World War, had taken their toll; so perhaps had the stability of the ground. In 1902 an Act of Parliament, the GWR (Crumlin Viaduct) Act, gave the railway for one year compulsory powers of purchase of the neighbouring coal mines, in order to enable them to secure the viaduct against injury. In 1928 the whole deck was replaced with steel and the track was singled using the up line. Now only one train at a time could use the bridge, and the speed limit was reduced to 8 m.p.h.. In July 1929 the single line was switched to the down side. Shortly afterwards it was slewed to the centre.

Thus it remained until closure. Those who drove trains across it say that it had a pronounced tendency to swing sideways under the weight of a train. One driver likened the motion to that of an Atlantic swell. The last train ran across it on 13 June 1964. After being featured in a film called *Arabesque* which starred Sophia Loren, it was pulled down in 1965. The masonry abutments which remain bear silent and breath-taking testimony to a daring piece of Victorian engineering.

A passenger on the Western Valley line, standing on the platform at Crumlin Low Level and looking up at a train on the viaduct 200 ft above, may well have wondered why it was built so high. Almost certainly it had been decided that the long incline up the Glyn valley from Pontypool was unavoidable, but that, having attained that altitude, it was desirable to maintain it for as great a distance as possible, in order to minimise the gradients for loaded trains moving towards the east. The choice of an iron girder bridge at Crumlin was almost certainly made on grounds of cost; it is less clear why the Hengoed viaduct was nevertheless built of masonry.

Two pannier tanks and two brake vans make their way west towards the Glyn Tunnel. August 1963.

Alan Jarvis.

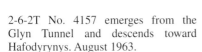

2-6-2T No. 4157 emerges from the Glyn Tunnel and descends toward Hafodyrynys. August 1963.

Alan Jarvis.

FROM THE EBBW TO THE LLWYD

The final section of this description starts with a climb through a trough in the hillside high above the Ebbw valley. Just beyond the viaduct, the single track Llanhilleth branch entered on the left having climbed at 1 in 40 up from the valley floor. The main line then climbed past Hafodyrynys Platform, installed in 1913 to serve a colliery, and into the Glyn Tunnel, 280 yds long. After a further short climb the summit was reached at Cefn Crib signal box before the descent of the Glyn Bank. This long decline at 1 in 45 initially wound its way through wood and mountain scenery, interspersed with collieries; here the railway, sidings and works were all squeezed into the narrow valley which had so impressed Coxe in 1799, while the steep hillside on the south side was streaked with the zig-zag lines of mineral tramways feeding into the main line. Shortly before Pontypool Clarence Street station, built by Liddell and located near the end of a straight stretch of the bank, the former Monmouthshire Railway Eastern Valleys branch crossed overhead; a link line was put in some time before 1882 at what was known as Trosnant Junction. The down platform at Clarence Street had the additional so-called Third Line running behind it.

Hafodyrynys Platform, looking east and up towards the Glyn Tunnel, just visible in the distance. May 1960.
N. D. Mundy.

Eastern portal of the Glyn Tunnel. June 1964.
R. H. Marrows.

A colliers' platform in the Glyn Valley looking downhill towards Pontypool. Although the Vale of Neath Line was closed to passengers from June 1964, this part of the line was still open for coal traffic in April 1965.

R. H. Marrows.

Hafodyrynys Colliery looking west. April 1964.

R. H. Marrows.

The view westward up the
Glyn Valley from Clarence
Street Station showing
Trosnant Junction Signal
Box on the Eastern Valley
line, which here crossed
over the TVE. June 1963.
J. Stone.

Clarence Street
Station, looking
west, with the
path of the
so-called Third
Line in the left
fore-ground.
December 1963.
R. H. Marrows.

No. 7230 joins the TVE west of Clarence Street having left
the Eastern Valley line at Trosnant Junction. c. 1963.
W. Spurrier.

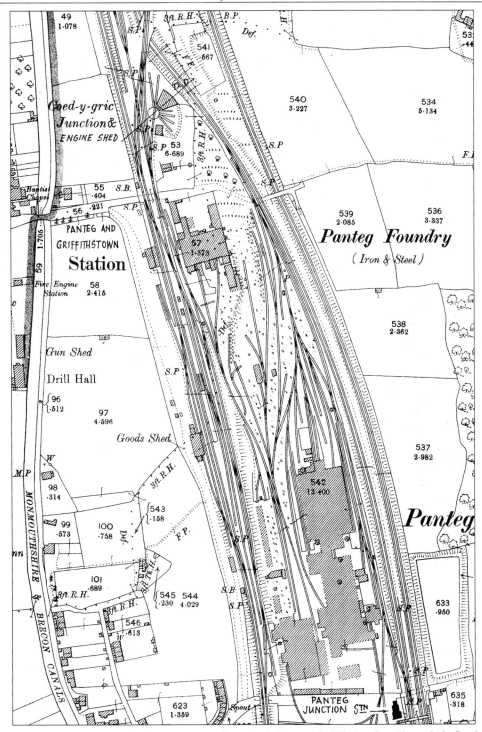

The southern end of the Pontypool Road complex from the O.S. map of 1882 showing: *Upper Left:* Coed-y-gric Junction; the first locomotive shed still in existence; and Panteg & Griffithstown Station. *Centre:* the Pontypool, Caerleon and Newport (PCN) Line built in September 1874 to convey freight direct from the TVE to Newport, by-passing the MRCC. *Extreme right:* the December 1874 PCN passenger line from Pontypool Road Station to Newport. *Lower right:* Panteg Junction Station.

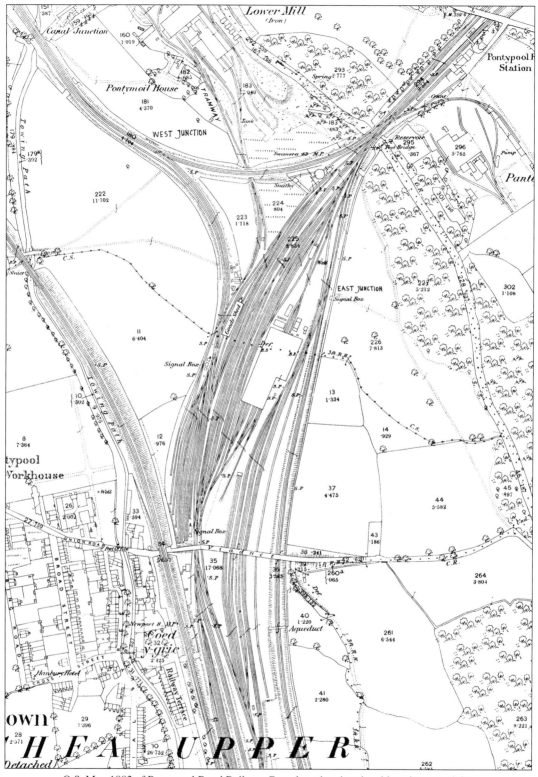

O.S. Map 1882 of Pontypool Road Railway Complex, showing the old station, top right.

Crown Copyright.

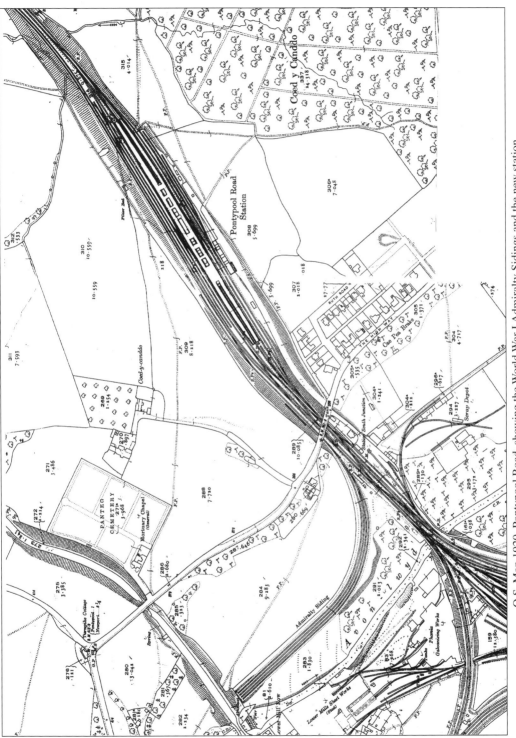

O.S. Map 1920, Pontypool Road, showing the World War I Admiralty Sidings and the new station.

As the Glyn valley opened out at its confluence with the Afon Llwyd, the line came in sight of the great railway complex of Pontypool Road. Here the sidings and works were within a vast triangle of lines. It will be recalled that the NAH had been authorised by Parliament to construct a railway northward to Hereford from a junction with the Newport to Pontypool line of the Monmouthshire Railway. This point, known as Coed-y-gric Junction, lay at the southern end of the triangle. The old MRCC line ran northward past this junction and to the west of the complex of sidings, and passed over the TVE at Trosnant Crossing on its way to Pontypool Crane Street station and the Eastern Valley. The third point of the triangle, to the north and east, where the TVE left the Hereford line, was known as Taff Vale Extension Junction or West Junction. The original engine shed, located in the southern angle of track near Coed-y-gric Junction, was replaced gradually by a much larger series of buildings located close to the centre of the triangle of track. First a round-house was built, and then an additional straight shed was added to the south of it. These survived until 1967. Adjacent to them lay the coal stage, greatly increased in size in 1897, and capable of coaling the largest locomotives. The sidings were extended progressively to tackle the increasing traffic. Trains were marshalled at Pontypool Road; iron and coke for Dudley and south Staffordshire, or steam coal for shipping at Birkenhead. The so-called 'middle' sidings handled traffic for Staffordshire, Birmingham

An uncommon and impressive view of the sidings and engine sheds at Pontypool Road, looking north-east.
R.H. Marrows Collection.

A similar view of Pontypool Road engine sheds and sidings in decay, April 1967.
R. H. Marrows.

Pontypool Road Shed in its heyday I: R.O.D. 2-8-0 No. 3023. May 1936.
F. K. Davies.

Pontypool Road Shed in its heyday II: 2-6-2T No. 4504. September 1937.
F. K. Davies.

and London, whilst the 'Birkenhead' sidings held traffic for Shrewsbury, Chester, Manchester and Birkenhead; the 'east' and 'Coed-y-gric' sidings attracted the incoming empties and goods traffic for the TVE and the Western valleys via Llanhilleth. A typical goods train from Manchester on 4 November 1879 had two waggons for Pontypool Road, four for Swansea, one for Ebbw Vale, one for Cefn, three for Cardiff, one for Aberdare, three for Whitland, two for Llanelly, one for Bridgend, one for Haverfordwest, two for Neath, one for Carmarthen, one for Newport, one for Pontypool, two for Neath Abbey, one for Briton Ferry, and one for Aberbeeg. These were sorted and on their way in 30 minutes. Until the late '20s a Transfer Shed received composite loads, which were emptied out on to the shed floor and made up into full waggon loads for onward transmission. The employment thus generated contributed to the expansion of Pontypool and led to the creation of the terraced villages of Sebastopol and Griffithstown; the latter being the creation of the first station master at Pontypool Road, Henry Griffiths, who set up a co-operative building society to provide housing.

The original passenger station was immediately south of the present one and of the road bridge, but just north of where the TVE bore away from the main line to the west. It was of stone, with gables and chimneys in the style of Liddell's other stations on the line. It consisted of, on the east side, a station master's house, (which survives as a private house), and a platform with offices and a small south facing bay. On the west side of the main line there was a simple island platform which served trains on the TVE. At the time of opening in January 1854, the LNWR, as operators, named it Newport Road, presumably in deference to the first town in the title of the NAH, but it was clearly stretching a point and by May the name had become Pontypool Road. By the turn of the century the station had become congested and, in 1909, was replaced by a new station constructed north of the road bridge. This comprised a large island platform with two inset bays, the northern for the line to Monmouth, the southern for the TVE. The main entrance to the new station was through a plain brick building to the east of the main line, and then by way of a passage under the tracks. It was approached down a road sloping northward from the bridge over the railway. Traditional GW red and blue brick was the principle building material and there was a strong family resemblance to other GW stations, particularly Nelson & Llancaiach.

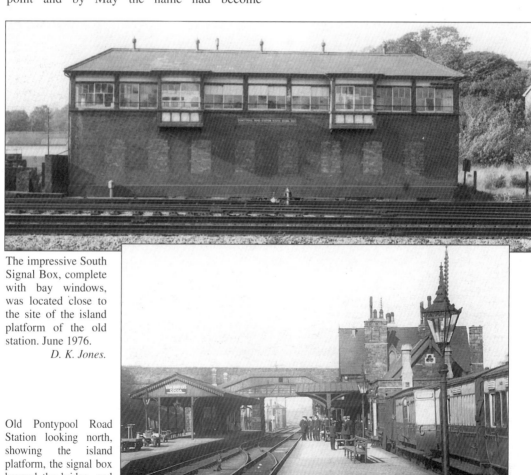

The impressive South Signal Box, complete with bay windows, was located close to the site of the island platform of the old station. June 1976.
D. K. Jones.

Old Pontypool Road Station looking north, showing the island platform, the signal box beyond the bridge, and some vintage carriages in the bay platform. No date.
R.H. Marrows Coll.

The new Pontypool Road station nearing completion in 1909, viewed from the west.
Torfaen Museum, Pontypool.

General view from the south of the new Station showing the signalling in a state of transition, 1909.
R.H. Marrows Coll.

Hawksworth pannier tank No. 8445 gets an involuntary bath in the Neath bay on 23 August 1958.
F. K. Davies.

Diesel Rail Car No. W30W in the Monmouth bay at the north end of Pontypool Road Station. No date.
R. W. A. Jones.

Pontypool Road Station looking south, showing the scissors cross-over and the platform edge, slightly indented, to accommodate the outside cylinders of GW locomotives. No date.
NMRW.

Vale of Neath bay at Pontypool Road. No date.
NMRW.

Pontypool Road Station from the station approach road I, ca. 1930.

V. R. Webster.

Pontypool Road Station from the station approach road II, ca 1964.

GBJ.

Pontypool Road Station from the station approach road III, immediately before the demolition of the booking office in November 1993.

DD.

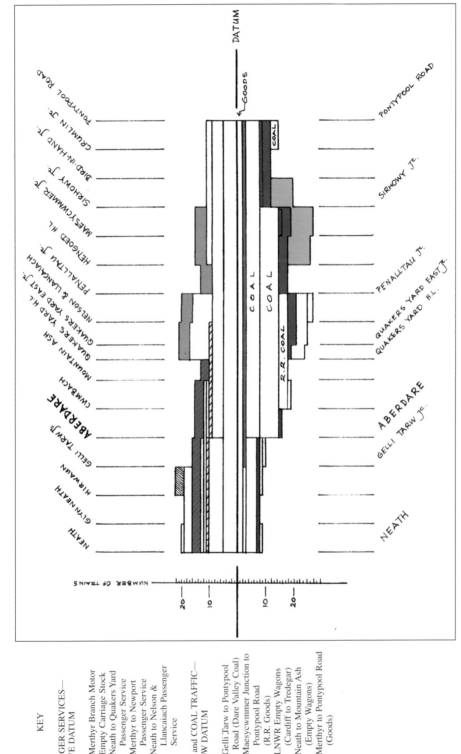

Flow and block diagram of up trains on the Vale of Neath Line in 1913. Passenger workings are shown above the datum line; those represented below are freight/coal trains. More than 100 trains in each direction were scheduled over all or part of the line. Note the relatively few covering the whole line, the break at Aberdare and the intensity between Quakers Yard and Penalltau Junction.

GBJ.

KEY

PASSENGER SERVICES—
ABOVE DATUM

Merthyr Branch Motor
Empty Carriage Stock
Neath to Quakers Yard
    Passenger Service
Merthyr to Newport
    Passenger Service
Neath to Nelson &
    Llancaiach Passenger
    Service

GOODS and COAL TRAFFIC—
BELOW DATUM

Gelli Tarw to Pontypool
    Road (Dare Valley Coal)
Maesycwmmer Junction to
    Pontypool Road
    (R.R. Goods)
LNWR Empty Wagons
    (Cardiff to Tredegar)
Neath to Mountain Ash
    (Empty Wagons)
Merthyr to Pontypool Road
    (Goods)

Chapter 5

OPERATIONS

From the completion of the Middle Duffryn link in 1864 until closure 100 years later, most of the traffic using the line from Neath to Pontypool Road operated only over parts of it. The flow diagram, which is derived from the Working Timetable, illustrates in broad terms the flow of up (eastbound) traffic, both goods and passenger in 1913. In south Wales it was general practice to describe up movements as those away from the ports and, as it generally happened, up the valleys. On the Vale of Neath Line, as was common elsewhere, up was towards London, i.e. eastbound, regardless of the gradient. However it had not always been so, as, for a period after the GWR took over, from 1867 until about 1870, the designations were reversed. This may have been because, until after 1872 and the narrowing of the gauge on the South Wales Railway, there was no direct connection between the old NAH line and the GWR at Newport; Neath was the only interchange station for a GWR passenger to London.

Because up was designated as the direction of London, where an up movement used part of the Neath to Pontypool line on its way up to a colliery, it was perfectly possible for an up train to be working in the down direction. For example, a train of empty coal waggons from Cardiff to Dowlais would proceed up the Rhymney to Penalltau Junction, at which point it would go down to Llancaiach and then up the joint line to Dowlais—uphill all the way.

1913 was the peak year for the coal trade, though not as it happens in the Aberdare area where it occurred earlier. However the picture is incomplete, as the diagram does not include all of the coal traffic destined for the Welsh ports, as most of the coal movements from the collieries to the docks were controlled from distribution centres by way of intermediate sidings, where the trains awaited call-forward to the dock; these movements were not all included in the working timetables.

PASSENGER TRAINS

When the VNR and NAH began operations, railway travel was still fairly primitive.

Comparatively few trains maintained the 40 to 50 m.p.h. then feasible for any length of time; most services were much slower, the journeys were long, and the carriages crowded, smelly, dusty, and generally uncomfortable. Nevertheless, passenger traffic across the country grew rapidly, for the cost was half that of the road carriage, and the journey time significantly shorter. Passenger traffic initially grew faster than goods with only in 1858 a brief set-back due to the economy, but, by the mid-fifties, it settled down to an overall 45 : 55 ratio in favour of goods. The proportion of goods traffic, mainly minerals, at 1 : 3 on the VNR was thus quite exceptional. The general slow start to goods traffic is attributed to the resistance of the canals and the absence of an adequate administrative system for allocating equitably the revenues arising from goods transferred between companies. This was gradually rectified following the creation in 1842 of the Railway Clearing House.

In 1844 Parliament had stipulated that at least one third class train a day in each direction should be operated on all lines and third class travel grew from a 41% share of travel in 1845 to 95% by the end of the century. In south Wales it was the practice either to make all trains available to 1st, 2nd, and 3rd class passengers, or to run the so-called Parliamentary train as a train for all three classes and the remainder for first and second class only.

Passenger trains started running on the VNR in 1851, on the NAH main line in 1854, on the TVE as far as Crumlin in 1855, and to Pontllanfraith (then Tredegar Junction) in 1857; it was not until 1858 that the first train ran as far as Quakers Yard.

In 1865 when the GWR had taken over and the Middle Duffryn link had been completed, there were three standard gauge trains a day in each direction from Hereford to Swansea. For passengers from the north it was no longer necessary to change trains at Pontypool Road; Merthyr on the other hand was now made a subsidiary destination, requiring a change of train at Quakers Yard for passengers to and from the east.

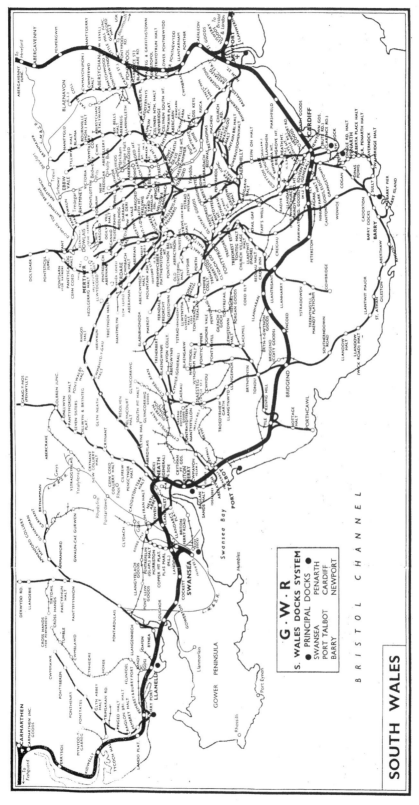

GWR timetable map of the railways of south-east Wales after the Grouping.

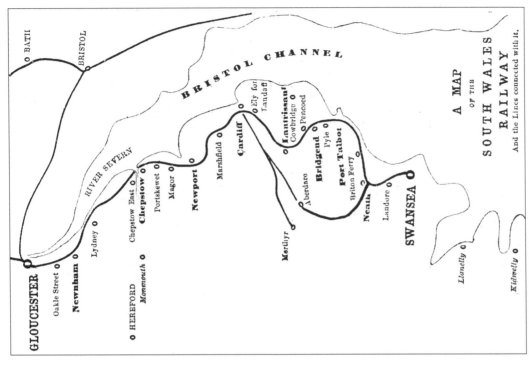

A MAP OF THE SOUTH WALES RAILWAY. And the Lines connected with it.

Malcolm James Coll.

VNR Map and Timetable, 1851. Note the bus connection for Merthyr, and the use of London Time. The Sunday extension of the bus to Dowlais covered the journey markedly quicker downhill!

VALE OF NEATH RAILWAY.

London Time is kept at all the Stations on this Railway, which is 15 minutes before Swansea Time, and 14 minutes before Merthyr Time.

Omnibuses run in connexion with each Train, between **Merthyr** and the **Merthyr Road Station**, on Sundays and Week Days, at the following Fares:—

Inside—Single Journey...... 1s. 0d. — Double Journey...... 1s. 9d.
Outside—Single Journey...... 0s. 10d. — Double Journey...... 1s. 6d.

Passengers to or from **London**, or any of the Intermediate Stations on the South Wales or Great Western Lines, will be re-booked at Neath.

Swansea, Neath, Hirwain, Aberdare, and Merthyr.

Dis-tance Mls	UP TRAINS. DEPARTURE FROM	WEEK DAYS 1,2 & Parl.	1,2 & Parl.	1,2 & Parl.	SUNDAYS 1,2 & Parl.	1,2 & Parl.	1,2 & Parl.	FARES 1st Class s. d.	2d Class s. d.	3d Class s. d.	CARRIAGES 4 wheel s. d.	2 wheel s. d.	HORSES Each s. d.	property at same per rd.
		A.M.	P.M.	P.M.	A.M.	P.M.	P.M.							
0	**Swansea,.**	7 45	2 0	7 0	9 0	6 0								
	Prt.Talbot ⎫ per South Wales				9 5	6 0	8 0							
	Briton-Ferry.. ⎬ Railway.				9 12	6 10	8 7							
8	**Neath..** arr.	8 5	2 25	7 25	9 20	6 20	8 15	1 6	1 0	0 8	6 6	5 0	5 6	8 6
	" dep.	8 13	2 30	7 30	9 25	6 30								
9¼	Aberdylais	8 19	2 36	7 36	9 31	6 36		2 0	1 4	0 10				
14½	Resolven	8 30	2 47	7 47	9 42	6 47	This Train *stops* at Neath Station.	2 8	1 10	1 2				
17	Glyn-Neath	8 39	2 56	7 56	9 51	6 56		3 4	2 0	1 5				
23½	**Hirwain**	9 8	3 26	8 26	10 20	7 25		4 6	3 0	2 0	12 0	9 0	11 0	16 6
24	Merthyr Road	9 15	3 30	8 30	10 27	7 32		4 8	3 2	2 0				
27	**Aberdare**	9 25	3 40	8 40	10 35	7 40		5 0	3 4	2 3	15 0	9 6	12 0	18 0
	Merthyr ⎫ Arrival per Omni-	10 20	4 35	9 35	11 30	9 35								
	Dowlais ⎬ bus from Merthyr Road Station...				12 0	10 0								

Merthyr, Aberdare, Hirwain, Neath, and Swansea.

Dis-tance Mls	DOWN TRAINS. DEPARTURE FROM	WEEK DAYS 1,2 & Parl.	1,2 & Parl.	1,2 & Parl.	SUNDAYS 1,2 & Parl.	1,2 & Parl.	1,2 & Parl.	FARES 1st Class s. d.	2d Class s. d.	3d Class s. d.	CARRIAGES 4 wheel s. d.	2 wheel s. d.	HORSES Each s. d.	property at same per rd.
		A.M.	P.M.	P.M.	A.M.	A.M.	P.M.							
	Dowlais ⎫ Per Omnibus for					7 30	4 50							
	Merthyr ⎬ Merthyr Road Station.	7 45	1 10	5 20		7 45	5 10							
0	**Aberdare**	8 35	2 0	6 10		8 35	6 0							
2¾	Merthyr Road	8 49	2 14	6 24		8 47	6 14	0 6	0 4	0 2				
3½	**Hirwain**	8 55	2 20	6 30		8 53	6 20	0 8	0 6	0 3	5 6	4 0	4 6	6 6
9	Glyn-Neath	9 17	2 42	6 50		9 15	6 40	2 0	1 4	0 10				
12½	Resolven	9 28	2 53	7 1		9 24	6 51	2 8	1 8	1 0				
17½	Aberdylais	9 39	3 4	7 13		9 35	7 3	3 6	2 2	1 5				
19	**Neath....** arr.	9 43	3 8	7 18		9 40	7 8	3 8	2 4	1 7	10 6	8 0	9 6	14 0
	" dep.	9 45	3 10	7 20	8 30	9 45	7 15							
	Briton-Ferry .. ⎫ per Sth. Wales					9 52	7 22							
	Port Talbot ⎬ Railway.				8 45	10 0	7 30							
27	**Swansea,** arr.	10 15	3 35	7 45		10 5	7 35	5 0	3 4	2 3	13 0	9 6	12 0	18 0

ABERDARE, MERTHYR, HIRWAIN, and NEATH.—Vale of Neath.

VNR Timetable, January 1853. Journey times have been reduced.

PRO: RAIL 903.11.

MERTHYR, ABERDARE, HIRWAIN, and NEATH.—Vale of Neath.

VNR Timetable, December 1853. The Merthyr branch has been opened, reducing Aberdare to branch line status.

PRO: RAIL 903.11.

NAH Timetable, September 1855. The TVE has been opened as far as Crumlin; Euston is suggested as a London terminus.

PRO: RAIL 903.16.

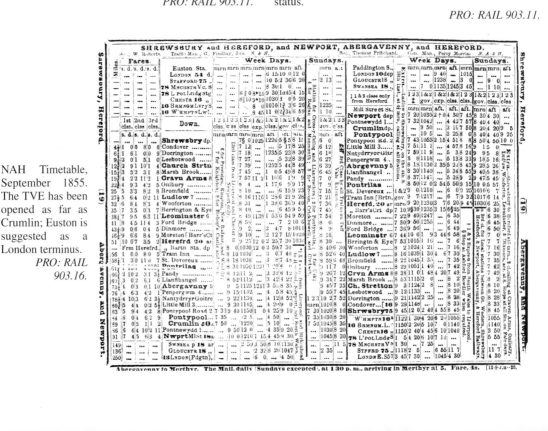

SHREWSBURY and HEREFORD, and NEWPORT, ABERGAVENNY, and HEREFORD.

Abergavenny to Merthyr. The Mail daily (Sundays excepted) at 1 30 p.m., arriving in Merthyr at 5, Fare, 4s.

Abergavenny to Merthyr.—The "Royal Mail," on Week Days, at 1 8/p.m., arriving at 5 p.m. (Fare, 4s.); waits the 120 exp.

SHREWSBURY and HEREFORD, and NEWPORT, ABERGAVENNY, and HEREFORD.

Sec., W. Roberts. Traffic Man., G. Findlay, Jun. S. & B.   Sec. Thomas Pritchard. Gen. Man., Percy Morris. N.A. & H.

(Detailed timetable for Shrewsbury and Hereford, Newport, Abergavenny routes — Down and Up directions, Week Days and Sundays. Stations listed include Shrewsbury, Condover, Dorrington, Leebotwood, Church Stretton, Marsh Brook, Craven Arms, Onibury, Bromfield, Ludlow, Woferton, Berrington & Eye, Leominster, Ford Bridge, Dinmore, Moreton, Hereford, Tram Inn, Pontrilas, St. Devereux, Abergavenny, Penpergwm, Nantyderry or Goitre, Usk, Llanbadoc, Pandy, Pontypool, Newport, Crumlin, Tredegar, Mill Street Sta.)

NAH Timetable, 1857. The TVE has been opened as far as Tredegar Junction, also called, for a time, Blackwood.

PRO: RAIL 903.19.

Shrewsbury, Hereford,   (19)   Abergavenny and Newport.

COLEFORD, MONMOUTH, USK and PONTYPOOL. (Traffic Man., W. Lane.)

(Timetable detail — Up and Down, Week Days and Sundays, stations including Newport, Pontnewydd, Pontypool Road, Little Mill, Usk, Llandenny, Raglan Road, Dingestow, Monmouth)

(Lower portion: Shrewsbury & Hereford, Newport, Abergavenny & Hereford full timetable)

Shrewsbury, Hereford.   (19)   Abergavenny, and Newport.

NAH Timetable, January 1858. The TVE is at last open to Quakers Yard, with two through trains per day to Merthyr.

PRO: RAIL 903.20.

Shrewsbury, Hereford,   (19)   Abergavenny and Newport.

COLEFORD, MONMOUTH, USK and PONTYPOOL. (Traffic Man., W. Lane.)

(Timetable detail similar to left, March 1858)

Shrewsbury, Hereford,   (19)   Abergavenny and Newport.

NAH Timetable, March 1858. Timings at Quakers Yard suggest that some trains operate through to Merthyr.

PRO: RAIL 903.20

No. 4.

TAFF VALE AND ABERDARE EXTENSIONS.

DOWN.

	1 Empties.	2 Empties.	3 Minerals.	4 Empties.	5 Empties.	6 Thro' Dud.y Minerals.	7 Coal. Empties.	8 Pick Up.	9 Empties.	10 Empties fr. Paddington.	11 Empties.	12 Goods.	13 Passenger.	14 Empties.	15 Hereford Coal	16 Minerals & Empties.
	p.m.	p.m.	a.m.	a.m.	a.m.	a.m.	a.m.	a.m.	a.m.	a.m.	a.m.	a.m.	a.m.	a.m.	a.m.	
Pontypool Road	dep. 10 0	10 12								8 30	8 30	9 30		10 10		R
Pontypool	arr. 10 12							6 30	R			9 10	10 5	10 10	11 5	
Ponda Siding	dep.													10 10		
Blaendare Siding														10 40	11 25	11 30
Cefn Crib Siding	arr.															11 46
Crumlin	dep. 10 30	12 30		2 30			5 30	7 10				10 0	10 28	10 50		11 55
Llanhilleth	dep.					5 30		7 25								
	dep.							7 35								
Tredegar Junction	arr.				4 50	5 45	5 50	7 40	6 30			10 20	10 30	11 0		12 6
Sirhowy Junction	dep. 10 50	12 50	2 50	3 50			6 46	7 50	7 0			10 40	10 41	11 20		12 15
Maesycwmmer Siding	arr.							8 0	7 15							
Rhymney Junction	dep.							8 10	7 25							
Penallta	arr.		3 30	4 20			6 20	8 20	7 40	9 20	9 50	11 10	10 49	11 35		12 47
	dep. 11 30		3 40	4 45			6 25	8 30	7 50	9 35		11 15	5 10 55		11 35	1 30
Llancaich	arr. 11 40		4 5	5 6			6 45	8 35	8 0			11 20	11 6			1 40
Quaker's Yard	arr.							8 40	8 10			11 30				1 45
Mountain Ash	dep.							8 50	8 15	9 0		12 5	11 25			2 25
Middle Duffryn	arr.							9 0	9 10	9 10		12 20				2 40
Aberdare												12 30 11 25				
Hirwain	arr.											12 40 11 46				
Hirwain Ponds	dep.											12 15				
Glyn Neath																
Resolven	arr.											1 50	11 64			
Aberdylais	d-p.											2 0	12 5			
Neath Junction	dep.															
Neath	arr.											CR 12 10				
Briton Ferry Road	dep.											2 30 12 22				
Swansea	arr.											2 30 12 35				
Quaker's Yard	dep.							6 30	9 55				10 51			
Troedyrhiew	arr.												11 0			
Merthyr	arr.												11 8			

The Pontypool Road Engines will call at Tredegar Junction when required to pick up.

Special Trains will be run between Pontypool Road and Quaker's Yard when required.

No. 11 will leave Traffic at Maesycwmmer when required.

When Nos. 6 and 8 Down Trains are light, they will take on the Lancaich Empties from Tredegar Junction.

No. 12 must shunt at Rhymney Junction for No. 13 Down Passenger Train to pass.

The Engine to work No. 9 Train, leaves Pontypool Road coupled to No. 4 Train.

No. 16. **R** to run when required.

No. 9. **R** to run when required only between Blaendare and Rhymney Junction.

No. 12. **CR** to call at Crumlin Junction and Neath Abbey when required by Signal.

No. 4.

GREAT WESTERN RAILWAY.

SERVICE TIME TABLES,

PRINTED FOR THE

USE OF THE COMPANY'S SERVANTS.

WEST MIDLAND SECTION.

Oxford to Worcester, Wolverhampton, Hereford, and Newport;

Including the Witney, Bourton-on-the-Water, Chipping Norton, Severn Valley, Much Wenlock, Stourbridge and Monmouth Branches, and the Taff Vale and Aberdare Extensions.

June, 1865.

AND UNTIL FURTHER NOTICE.

The Time specified in the Time Tables is the Departure of Passenger Trains and the *passing* time of Goods Trains, when the times of arrival and departure are not stated; and in all cases the Trains should *arrive* in sufficient time to enable the work to be done, in order to leave the Station at the appointed hour.

LONDON:

PRINTED BY HENRY TUCK.

Sample page from the June 1865 working timetable for what was then termed the West Midland Section.

We know from an accident report of 1866, when a passenger train from Swansea to Hereford collided with a goods train just north of Aberdare, that a typical train at this time consisted of a tank engine, a 1st class carriage, a 2nd, a 3rd, and a composite, all without brakes, and two brake vans. The driver of this particular train alleged that he was descending to Aberdare from Hirwaun at the moderate speed of 20 m.p.h., but a frightened passenger was sure it was over 30 m.p.h.

As to the appearance of these early trains, records are incomplete, and some characteristics are disputed. The livery of the VNR locomotives was dark green and similar to the contemporary Great Western; the first class carriages were grey with black above the waist line; interior upholstery was red; the other carriages were a creamy grey. The livery of the NAH is less certain. Pritchard in his *Railways of S.E. Monmouthshire* refers to a passenger locomotive livery of brown with gold lining, with brass boiler mountings and splashers. There is some likelihood that the goods locomotives were green, as the first were formerly the property of T. Brassey and green was usually his preferred colour. In the absence of evidence to the contrary

it seems likely that the carriages were brown. The West Midland followed the OWW in using dark green for the locomotives above the footplate, with black for the smokebox and chimney. The wheels were green and the frames red-brown; boiler bands were black with a thin red line either side; a similar black band edged the body panels with a red line inside it. Buffer beams were red. Carriages seemingly were a darker brown than the contemporary GWR; the accompanying photograph shows the characteristic curved moulding and distinctive gold lettering.

On the old VNR (which had no standard gauge carriages) one broad gauge train a day in each direction ran from Aberdare and from Merthyr to Swansea Wind Street between 1864 and 1872. The broad gauge also made a connection for Merthyr with the Hereford trains at Hirwaun. By 1913 there were five trains between Swansea and Pontypool Road, Hereford having been dropped from direct connection in April 1873. Sometime between 1872 when the VNR had become standard gauge and 1889, the GWR demoted Merthyr to branch status, serving it by a train terminating at Hirwaun. This provoked a 'Memorial' from the Mayor,

The engineer's drawing of the Hengoed Viaduct on page 79 contains a finely sketched illustration of a NAH mixed train of ca. 1857.

PRO: RAIL 513.16.

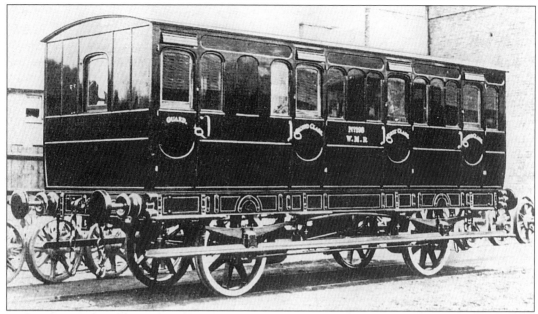

The maker's photograph of a West Midland carriage showing the characteristic curved moulding.

HMRS.

Weak winter sunshine and the Merthyr auto-train at Abernant in November 1963.

John Davies.

The Merthyr auto-train leaves Abernant for Hirwaun. November 1963.

John Davies.

Aldermen and Burgesses of Swansea, complaining to the GWR that there were no fast trains to Merthyr, that there were in any case only five a day compared with twelve from Cardiff on the TVR, that the carriages were old and dirty, and that trains were frequently delayed waiting for connections from London. Ten years later, for a short period, a Merthyr to Swansea train operated with limited stops; it was something of an express although taking 70 minutes for the journey, which is perhaps the reason why it was dropped in 1902. That seems to have been the only action taken until October 1908, when second-class travel was abolished on the line.

Edwardian passenger train near Gelli Tarw, photographed against the afternoon sun, but showing stock typical of the period, and drawn by one of the ubiquitous GW saddle-tanks. ca. 1906.

Ivor J. John.

Steam Rail Motor No. 7 at Resolven down platform. No date.

R. W. Kidner Coll.

Great Western 70ft Steam Rail Motor No. 37 standing at Neath Riverside Station. No date.
Stephenson Locomotive Society Collection.

Victorian carriages stand in the Vale of Neath bay at Pontypool Road. June 1922.
E. T. Miller, courtesy D. K. Jones.

By 1913 a variety of new trains had been introduced covering part only of the line. The GW/RR joint line from Merthyr to Quakers Yard High Level down the west side of the Taff vale had been opened in 1886. At Penalltau Junction trains from this line branched southward down the valley of the Rhymney river to Ystrad Mynach, Caerphilly, and Cardiff. There were five a day in each direction. From 1906 until the start of the First World War there was another service, operated by rail-cars, from Merthyr over the joint line and then along the Vale of Neath line as far as the Sirhowy valley and so to Newport. The other GW/RR joint line, from Dowlais, joined the Pontypool line at Llancaiach, although most of these trains terminated there. Three trains ran from Aberdare to Pontypool Road. On Sundays there was no goods traffic and three trains only ran, one continuing beyond Swansea to Carmarthen. There was also considerable excursion traffic, in the summer to the seaside and in winter for football matches. The effect of this traffic on the line was noticeable between Tredegar Junction and Hengoed as there was quite a demand for trips to Barry Island from Tredegar, for which the LNWR exercised its running rights over the RR and the Barry Railway.

During the first World War there was a slight reduction in the frequency of passenger trains, one Swansea and one Aberdare service being suspended. Thereafter train frequency recovered and reached a peak in the thirties, with six through trains a day from 1921, and eight by 1939. In 1923 a rail motor service was introduced from Ystrad Mynach to Swansea East Dock. Later cut back to Neath Riverside, the service survived until closure in 1964. In 1927 an auto train service was introduced on the branch known as 'Hall's Road' northward from Penar Junction towards Oakdale colliery. Oakdale and Penmaen Halts were under the supervision of the station master at Penar Junction, and another halt was established at Treowen on the main line between Penar Junction and Crumlin; a service operated between Pontypool Road and Oakdale for a few years, until Oakdale was closed in 1932 and Penmaen in 1939.

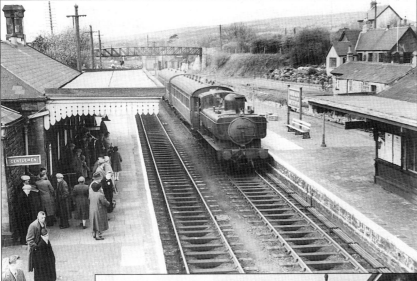

An interesting group of passengers wait on the down platform at Hirwaun for a Neath train, while 0-6-0PT No. 6433 stands at the island platform with a connecting service to Merthyr. 13 June 1957.

Ian L. Wright.

Hengoed Station approach: High Level, left; Low Level, right. June 1964.

J. Stone.

Merthyr auto-train near Gelli Tarw. July 1962. *Glyn Davies.*

0-6-0PT No. 6416 and auto-trailer form the 4.25 p.m. Merthyr service, leaving Hirwaun. 21 August 1962.
G. T. Robinson.

A writer in the *Railway Observer* for January 1937 gives a stimulating description of a ride on the Vale of Neath Line in an auto train powered by a pannier tank of the '6400' class. 'One brilliant Sunday morning in July 1935, I travelled on the 08.23 from Pontypool Road to Quakers Yard. 6400 itself was pushing one car (containing driver, guard, and myself) and for

the first few miles contented itself with a Wagnerian display on the exhaust. After Hafodyrynys (where the load was considerably augmented by the addition of numerous church-goers) 6400 treated me to one of the most terrifying journeys I have yet experienced, culminating with a maximum of 53 m.p.h. somewhere before Pentwynmawr, and 51 m.p.h.

PONTYPOOL, MERTHYR, ABERDARE AND NEATH. 73

Week Days only.

	a.m	a.m	a.m	p.m	a.m	a.m	a.m	p.m	p.m	p.m	p.m	p.m	p.m	p.m	p.m	p.m	p.m
PONTYPOOL ROAD dep.	8 40		7 45	8 26		8 40	11 8		1 15	2 28	4 0		4 0		6 20		
Pontypool (Clarence St.) „	8 44		7 50			8 46	11 5		1 19	2 33					6 25	8 10	
Hafodyrynys Platform „	6 56		8 0			8 57	11 15		1 29	2 42					6 34	8 15	
Crumlin (High Level) „			8 5			9 1	11 20		1 33	2 47					6 39	8 19	
Treowen Halt „	7 2																
Pentwynmawr Platform „	7 4		8 9			9 5	11 24		1 37	2 50		4 27			6 42	8 24	
Pontllanfraith „	7 9		8 12			9 7	11 27		1 40	2 53		4 30			6 45		
Hengoed (High Level) { arr.	7 13		8 16			9 11	11 31		1 44	2 58		4 35			6 48	8 31	
{ dep.	7 14		8 17			9 12	11 36		1 45	3 0		4 36			6 49	8 33	
Nelson and Llancaiach arr.	6 23	7 20	8 23			9 18	11 42		1 50	3 5		4 45			6 55	8 39	
Cardiff (Queen St.) dep.	5 12		6 38			8 15	10 8				3 15				5 30	7 30	
Ystrad Mynach „	5 52		7 20			8 55	10 43				2 34				6 11	8 1	
Nelson and Llancaiach dep.		7 28	8 24			9 19	11 43		1 51	3 6	3 59				6 44	8 40	
Trelewis Halt „		7 30	8 27			9 22	11 46		1 54	3 9	4 2				6 47	8 43	
Treharris „		7 34	8 30			9 25	11 49		1 56	3 11	4 5				6 50	8 46	
Quaker's Yard (High L'v'l) arr.		7 36	8 32			9 27	11 51		1 58	3 13	4 7				7 2	8 49	
Quaker's Yard (H. L.) dep.						11 0	12 10				4 8				7 10		
Pontygwaith Halt „						11 4	12 14				4 11				7 13		
Aberfan „						11 7	12 18				4 15				7 16		
Troedyrhiw Halt „						11 12	12 22				4 19				7 21		
Abercanaid „						11 16	12 26				4 23				7 31		
Merthyr arr.						11 21	12 32				4 29				8 13		
Quaker's Yard (High L.v'l) dep.		7 37	8 35			9 30	11 54		2 2	3 16	4 58			5 29	7 3	8 51	
Penrhiwceiber (High Level) „		7 41	8 40			9 34	11 59		2 7	3 21	5 31			5 34	8	8 56	
Mountain Ash (Cardiff Rd) „		7 45	8 44			9 38	12 3		2 16	3 24	5 7			5 37	7 12	9 0	
Cwmbach „		7 49				9 42	12 7		2 14	3 31	5 11				7 17		
Aberdare (H. Level) { arr.		7 53	8 52			9 46	12 15		2 19	3 34	5 15			5 48	7 21	9 8	
{ dep.		8 5				9 47	12 15		2 20	3 33					7 33		
Trecynon Halt „		8 8							2 26						7 45		
Hirwaun „ arr.		8 15				9 58	12 23		2 32	3 48							
Merthyr dep.		7 45				9 30	11 53		2 0	3 19					7 15		
Hirwaun dep.		8 16				10 0	12 25		2 33	3 52					7 47		
Rhigos Halt „		8 21							2 38								
Pontwalby Halt „		8 29							2 45								
Glyn Neath „		8 34				10 14	12 39		2 51	4 16					8 1	10 25	
Resolven „		8 40				10 20	12 45		2 57	4 12					8 7	10 30	
Melyncourt Halt „		8 43				10 24											
Clyne Halt „		8 46				10 27			3 3								
Aberdylais „		8 51				10 32	12 53		3 9	4 21					8 15	10 29	
NEATH (General) arr.		8 55				10 36	12 57		3 13	4 25					8 20	10 43	

	a.m	a.m	a.m	a.m	a.m	a.m	p.m	p.m	p.m	p.m	p.m	p.m	p.m	p.m
NEATH (General) dep.					7 40			11 32	1 35		3 45	4 20	5 50	9 48
Aberdylais „					7 45			11 37	1 40		3 50	4 24	5 56	9 53
Clyne Halt „									1 45			4 30		9 59
Melyncourt Halt „									1 48			4 33		10 2
Resolven „					7 53			11 45	1 51		3 58	4 37	6 4	10 8
Glyn Neath „					8 0			11 52	1 57		4 5	4 43	6 11	10 14
Pontwalby Halt „					8 5							4 49		
Rhigos Halt „												4 59		
Hirwaun „ arr.					8 19			12 10	2 16		4 22	5 4	6 28	
Merthyr arr.					8 42			12 41	2 46		4 51	5 29		
Hirwaun dep.					8 25			12 13	2 19		4 24	5 5	6 31	
Trecynon Halt „											4 31	5 12		
Aberdare (H. Level) { arr.					8 32			12 20	2 26		4 35	5 15	6 39	
{ dep.	6 25		7 50		8 34	11 40			2 23	3 56	4 37		6 48	
Cwmbach Halt „	6 29		7 54			11 44			2 32		4 41			
Mountain Ash (Cardiff Rd.) „	6 34		8 0		8 43	11 49			2 40	4 29	4 47		7 5	
Penrhiwceiber (High Level) „	6 37		8 4		8 47	11 54			2 40	4 33	4 51		7 5	
Quaker's Yard (High L'v'l) arr.	6 41		8 8		8 51	11 59			2 44	4 11	4 55		7 9	
Merthyr dep.					8 2	11 30		1 33		4 20			6 43	
Abercanaid „					8 8	11 35		1 39		4 24			6 48	
Troedyrhiw Halt „					8 12	11 38		1 43		4 28			6 52	
Aberfan „					8 18	11 43		1 47		4 32			6 57	
Pontygwaith Halt „					8 22	11 49		1 52		4 37			7 3	
Quaker's Yard (H. L.) arr.					8 25	11 51		1 53		4 39			7 5	
Quaker's Yard (High L'v'l) dep.	6 42		8 12	8 26	8 52	12 1	1 2	1 59		2 45	4 12	4 41	4 58	7 10
Treharris „	6 44		8 14	8 29	8 55	12 4	1 8			2 47	4 14	4 48	5 8	7 13
Trelewis Halt „	6 47		8 17	8 31	9 0	12 7	1 12			2 49	4 19	4 48	5 8	7 16
Nelson and Llancaiach arr.	6 48	8 11	8 19	8 34	9 0	12 9	1 9	12 17		2 52	4 19	4 51	5 6	7 14
Ystrad Mynach dep.	6 55	8 0	8 17		8 41					2 10	3 8	4 44		7 18
Cardiff (Queen St.) „	6 38	8 31	8 52		9 10					2 40	3 36	5 5	5 40	8 49
Nelson and Llancaiach dep.	5 54		7 45		8 20	9 1		12 10		2 53				7 19
Hengoed (High Level) { arr.	6 0		7 50		8 26	9 7		12 16		2 50	4 20		5 12	7 25
{ dep.			7 51		8 27	9 8				3 5	4 37		5 16	7 30
Pontllanfraith „			7 56		8 31	9 13		12 24		3 10	4 42		5 21	7 35
Pentwynmawr Platform „			7 58		8 34	9 16				3 13	4 44		5 21	7 38
Treowen Halt „			8 1											
Crumlin (High Level) „			8 4		8 38	9 20		12 30		3 18	4 49		5 28	7 42
Hafodyrynys Platform „			8 9		8 44	9 26				3 24	4 55		5 34	7 48
Pontypool (Clarence St.) „			8 18		8 53	9 35		12 44		3 34	5 5		5 43	7 57
PONTYPOOL ROAD arr.			8 57		9 39			12 48		3 38	5 9		5 48	8 6

For other trains between Cardiff, Quaker's Yard (High Level) and Merthyr, see pages 66 and 67.

NELSON & LLANCAIACH AND DOWLAIS. (Week Days only.)

	a.m	a.m	p.m	p.m		p.m	p.m	p.m			a.m	a.m	a.m	p.m	p.m	p.m
Nelson & Llancaiach dep.	6 35	9 56		3 15		5 48	8 25	10 15		**Dowlais** (Cae Harris) dep.	6 22	7 46	11 32	4 23	6 43	8 40
Trelewis Platform „	6 40	9 58		3 18		5 51	8 28	10 18		Cwm Bargoed „	5 32	7 54	11 41	4 32	6 52	8 49
Bedling „	7 6	10 6		3 26		5 59	8 37	10 26		Bedling „	5 40	8 2	11 49	4 40	7 0	8 57
Cwm Bargoed „	7 19	10 18		3 38		6 11	8 50	10 38		Trelewis Platform „	5 50	8 7	11 54	4 46	7 6	9 3
Dowlais (Cae Harris) arr.	7 27	10 27		3 47		6 29	8 59	10 47		**Nelson & Llancaiach** arr.	5 53	8 10	11 57	4 48	7 8	9 5

MERTHYR AND HIRWAUN.

Week Days only. (Third class only.)

	a.m	a.m	a.m	a.m	p.m		p.m	p.m	p.m	p.m	p.m	p.m			p.m	p.m	p.m	p.m
Merthyr dep.	6 55	7 45	9 30	11 53	1 15		2 0	3 19	4 54	5 45	7 15	8 10		**Hirwaun** dep.	8 21	10 5		12 20
Abernant „	7 4	7 54	9 42	12 3			2 6	3 24	5 3	5 54	7 24	8 30		Llwydcoed „	8 28	10 12		12 27
Llwydcoed „	7 8	7 58	9 46	12 6			2 13	3 32	5 7	5 58	7 28	8 35		Abernant „	8 33	10 17		12 31
Hirwaun arr.	8 8	9 53	12 14			9 21	3 39	5 14	6 5	7 35	8			**Merthyr** arr.	8 42	10 26		12 41

E—Arrives Neath (Riverside) Station.
G—Saturdays excepted.
H—Departs from Neath (Riverside) Station.
J—Via Hengoed. On Saturdays arr. Ystrad Mynach 5.19 p.m. and Cardiff (Queen Street) 6.35 p.m.
N—Via Hengoed. On Saturdays arr. Ystrad Mynach 7.38 p.m. and Cardiff (Queen Street) 8.3 p.m.
S—Saturdays only.
T—On Saturdays arrive 5.37 p.m.
W—Workmen's Train.
Y—Departure time.
Z—Arrival time.
§—Third class only.
:—Via Hengoed.
‡—Via Nelson and Llancaiach.

Sample page from the May 1944 GW passenger timetable.

GBJ Coll.

before the equally unpronounceable Pontllanfraith.' It is odd that he did not comment on the crossing of the Crumlin viaduct. Perhaps he had his eyes shut.

Once again war cut into passenger services. By 1942 there were only two through Swansea trains, and two for Neath. The other public trains were mainly auto trains. These ran from Aberdare or Llancaiach to Pontypool Road, Swansea to Aberdare or Mountain Ash, and Neath to Aberdare or Ystrad Mynach. Auto trains also operated the Merthyr to Cardiff service via Ystrad Mynach and the Merthyr branch from Hirwaun. The biggest change to the working timetable by 1942 was the introduction of a large number of workmen's trains. These reflected the war-time need of miners and factory workers to seek work further from their homes, as mines were extended and factories developed. These trains were timed to coincide with

shiftwork, so some started early in the morning. For instance, there was a 05.13 train at Hengoed from Ystrad Mynach to Pontypool Road. Shortly after there was a train from Brynmawr over the Llanhilleth branch (adapted for passenger working 24 February 1942) also to Pontypool, connecting with a train to the Glascoed ordnance factory near Usk. Indeed several special passenger trains a day used the Llanhilleth branch en route to Glascoed. More trains came from the Rhymney valley via Maesycwmmer Junction, which was adapted for passenger working 30 November 1941. Dowlais workmen were taken to Hengoed, whilst one early morning service operated from Neath Riverside to Quakers Yard H.L., and another from Glyn Neath to Merthyr. Thirteen trains were run to and from the Royal Ordnance Factory at Hirwaun each day, many being reversed in the nearby Rhigos carriage sidings.

0-6-0PT 9488 leaving Nelson and Llancaiach with the 3.55 p.m. Pontypool Road to Swansea train. Presumably no connection was intended with the 4.15 p.m. from Cae Harris, arriving with No. 5634. 13 March 1964.

G. T. Robinson.

Smoke and eary morning sunshine, as 2-6-2T No. 4169 heads the 7.45 a.m. Aberdare to Pontypool Road on 13 June 1964, the last day of passenger train operations on the Vale of Neath Line, and two days before final closure.

G. T. Robinson.

A double-headed Aberdare-bound train waits at Hirwaun with 0-6-0PTs 4688 and 3731. November 1963.

John Davies.

Tables 137–138

Table 137 PONTYPOOL ROAD, CARDIFF, ABERDARE, NEATH and SWANSEA

WEEK DAYS ONLY

Miles from Pontypool Rd.		am 𝔄		am	am 𝔄	am		am 𝔄		am	am 𝔄	am E		am J S		pm S 𝔄	pm S 𝔄		am E		am S
	164Newport .. .. dep	..	..	..	..	7 3	..	..	..	7 56	..	9 15	..	9 15	..	..	..	..	11 3	..	11N50
—	**Pontypool Road** ... dep	Workmen's Train	..	..	..	7 40	..	..	..	8 40	..	11 0	..	11 0	..	..	..	..	1p 5	..	1p 5
1¼	Pontypool **A**		..	..	..	7 44	..	..	..	8 44	..	11 4	..	11 4	..	..	..	..	1 9	..	1 9
5¼	Hafodyrynys Platform		..	..	..	..	..	..	..	8 56	..	11 14	..	11 14	..	..	..	..	1 19	..	1 19
6½	Grumlin (High Level) **B** ..		..	..	..	7 58	..	..	..	9 1	..	11 19	..	11 19	..	..	..	..	1 23	..	1 23
7¾	Pentwynmawr Platform...		..	..	..	..	..	..	..	..	..	..	..	..	..	..	..	..	..	..	..
9	Pontllanfraith (L.L.)		..	..	..	8 4	..	..	..	9 7	..	11 26	..	11 26	..	..	..	..	1 29	..	1 29
11	Hengoed (H.L.) **D**.... arr		..	..	..	8 9	..	..	..	9 11	..	11 30	..	11 30	..	..	..	..	1 33	..	1 33
—	Mls **Cardiff** (Q.St.) .. dep	5 15	..	..	6‡35	..	..	8 15	..	8 15	..	10 58	..	10 58	..	..	..	..	1 0	..	1 0
—	12¼ Ystrad Mynach	5 48	..	..	7 23	..	..	8 48	..	8 48	..	11 30	..	11 30	..	1235	..	..	1 33	..	1 33
—	13½ Hengoed (L.L.) **F** arr	5 52	..	..	..	..	..	8 50	..	8 50	..	11 33	..	11 33	..	..	..	..	1 35	..	1 35
—	Hengoed (H.L.)...... dep	6 30	..	..	..	8 17	..	8 58	..	9 16	..	11 35	..	11 35	..	..	..	..	1 44	..	1 44
14	**Nelson and Llancaiach** arr	6 36	..	..	7 30	8 23	..	9 4	..	9 21	..	11 41	..	11 41	..	1240	..	..	1 50	..	1 50
	Nelson and Llancaiach dep	6 45	..	..	7 33	8 24	..	..	..	9 22	9 35	11 42	..	11 42	..	1247	..	..	1 51	..	1 51
14¼	Trelewis Halt	To Dowlais (Cae Harris), arr 7 20 am (Table 139)	..	..	7 36	8 27	..	..	..	9 25	To Dowlais (Cae Harris) arr 10 7 am (Table 139)	11 45	..	11 45	..	To Dowlais (Cae Harris) arr 1 23 pm (Table 139)	..	..	1 53	..	1 53
15¼	Treharris		..	..	7 40	8 30	..	..	..	9 27		11 48	..	11 48	..		..	..	1 55	..	1 55
16	**Quaker's Yd.** (H.L.) **G** arr		..	..	**7 43**	**8 32**	..	..	..	**9 30**		**11 50**	..	**11 50**	..		..	..	**1 58**	..	**1 58**
22¾	125Merthyr ¶ ...... arr		..	..	8 8	8 55	..	..	..	10 45		12 42	..	12 42	..		..	..	2 42	..	2 42
—	**Quaker's Yd.** (H.L.). dep		..	..	7 45	8 35	..	..	..	9 32		11 53	..	11 53	..		1 12	..	2 2	..	2 2
17¾	Penrhiwceiber (H.L.)		..	..	7 50	8 40	..	..	..	9 37		11 57	..	11 57	..		1 16	..	2 6	..	2 6
19	Mountain Ash (Cardiff Rd.)		..	..	7 55	8 44	..	..	..	9 40		12 1	..	12 1	..		1 20	..	2 10	..	2 10
21½	Cwmbach Halt		..	..	7 59	8 48	..	..	..	9 44		12 5	..	12 5	..		1 24	..	2 14	..	2 14
22¾	**Aberdare** (H.L.) .. arr		..	..	**8 4**	**8 52**	..	..	..	**9 49**		**12 10**	..	**12 10**	..		**1 29**	..	**2 18**	..	**2 18**
	Aberdare (H.L.) .. dep		..	7 5	8 5	..	..	..	..	9 50		12 12	..	12 22	..		..	..	2 19	..	2 19
23¾	Trecynon Halt		..	7S 8	8 8	..	..	..	..	..		..	..	..	..		..	..	2 25	..	2 25
26½	Hirwaun .... arr		..	7 15	8 15	..	..	..	..	9 58		12 21	..	12 31	..		..	..	2 31	..	2 31
—	138Merthyr .. .. dep	..	..	6N50	..	..	..	..	..	9Z32	..	11C46	..	11N50	..	..	..	..	..	..	2N 5
—	Hirwaun .... dep	..	..	7 16	8 16	..	..	..	..	9 59	..	12 22	..	12 32	..	..	..	..	2 32	..	2 32
28¼	Rhigos Halt	..	..	7 23	8 21	..	..	..	..	..	..	..	..	..	..	..	..	..	2 37	..	2 37
31	Pontwalby Halt.........	..	..	..	8 29	..	..	..	..	..	..	..	..	..	..	..	..	..	2 44	..	2 44
32¾	Glyn Neath	..	..	7 40	8 34	..	..	..	..	10 13	..	12 38	..	12 47	..	..	..	..	2 49	..	2 49
35¼	Resolven	..	..	7 46	8 40	..	..	..	..	10 19	..	12 44	..	12 55	..	..	..	..	2 55	..	2 55
36½	Melyncourt Halt	..	..	..	8 43	..	..	..	..	..	..	..	..	..	..	..	..	..	2 59	..	2 59
37¾	Clyne Halt	..	..	..	8 46	..	..	..	..	..	..	..	..	..	..	..	..	..	3 2	..	3 2
40	Aberdylais Halt..	..	..	7 54	8 51	..	..	..	..	..	..	12 53	..	1 4	..	..	..	..	3 7	..	3 7
41¾	**Neath** (General) .... arr	..	..	**7 58**	**8L55**	..	..	..	..	**10 33**	..	**12 57**	..	**1 10**	..	..	..	..	**3 12**	..	**3 12**
49½	**104Swansea** (H. St.) . arr	..	..	**8 27**	**9§40**	..	..	..	..	**11 5**	..	**1 24**	..	**1 37**	..	..	..	..	**3 56**	..	**3 45**

For Notes, see page 261

Table 138 MERTHYR and HIRWAUN

WEEK DAYS ONLY—(Second class only)

Miles		am	am S	am F	am S		pm S		pm E		pm		pm		pm P	
—	**Merthyr** .. .. .. dep	6 50	9 32	1146	1150	..	2 5	..	3 19	..	4 54	..	5 40	..	7 25	..
3¼	Abernant	6 59	9 42	1154	1159	..	2 15	..	3 28	..	5 3	..	5 49	..	7 34	..
5½	Llwydcoed	7 3	9 47	12 0	12 4	..	2 20	..	3 33	..	5 7	..	5 53	..	7 39	..
7¼	**Hirwaun**........... arr	7 10	9 53	12 6	1210	..	2 26	..	3 39	..	5 14	..	6 0	..	7 45	..

Miles		am	am	am S		pm F	pm S	pm S		pm E		pm S		pm E	pm	pm P
—	**Hirwaun** .. .. .. dep	7 20	8 21	1010	..	1215	1220	2 35	..	4 25	..	5 24	..	5 54	6 50	8 14
2	Llwydcoed	7 29	8 28	1017	..	1222	1227	2 42	..	4 31	..	5 31	..	6 0	6 57	8 21
3¾	Abernant	7 33	8 33	1022	..	1227	1232	2 47	..	4 35	..	5 34	..	6 5	7 2	8 25
7¼	**Merthyr** .... arr	7 44	8 43	1031	..	1236	1243	2 57	..	4 48	..	5 45	..	6 15	7 12	8 35

E Except Saturdays
F Fridays only
P Runs Tuesdays, Wednesdays and Thursdays only
S Saturdays only

Sample page from the September 1961 BR passenger timetable.

GBJ Coll.

In 1951 the former GW/RR line from Merthyr to Quakers Yard had to be closed as subsidence had rendered the viaduct over the Taff unsafe. From that time the Cardiff service via the Rhymney valley started from Quakers Yard and passengers to and from Merthyr had to change between High and Low level. By 1956 there were five trains each way between Neath and Pontypool Road, two of which were extended to Swansea. There were still some workmen's trains and auto trains serving intermediate stations on the main line. Such was the general pattern until closure in 1964.

In his *GWR in the Twentieth Century*, O.S. Nock recalled an interesting journey over part of the line in an engineer's inspection saloon. After travelling from Cardiff up the Taff Vale line the party disembarked at Quakers Yard Low Level; while they went to inspect the site of the Penydarren Tramroad, the train was reversed up to Quakers Yard East on the Pontypool line, and then run forward into High Level station. Here the party rejoined the train and proceeded westward, through Aberdare as far as Gelli Tarw Junction. There they reversed again, passed through the Merthyr tunnel, and entered Merthyr over the old VNR line.

0-6-2T No. 6677 at Trelewis Halt, photographed on 21 July 1961; it appears that someone had been at pains to point out that the locomotive had not been painted for at least 13 years and to identify its former owners. The carriage is one of the GW's special excursion stock of 1938, an example of the variety of rolling stock engaged on the Vale of Neath line.

S. A. Leleux.

GOODS TRAINS

It is hard to find comprehensive information on early freight operations. For 1865 we have the evidence of the Working Timetables, which show that there were six coal trains from Mountain Ash to Pontypool Road during the morning, the first being just after midnight. These trains were probably a continuation of NAH and West MR schedules, as Mountain Ash is east of the Middle Duffryn link put in place

only a year previously. Two of these trains continued to Birkenhead, with one timetabled to south Staffordshire. Merthyr also despatched a train for this area and another for Manchester. There was also one through goods train from Swansea to Manchester, with another to Birmingham, and one from Aberdare to London, the latter being coal for the Great Western's own consumption. Joshua Williams had urged this movement on the GW when arguing the merits of their purchasing the VNR; routing over the VNR/TVE enabled standard gauge trains to be moved directly from Aberdare to London, avoiding the need to invest in mixing the gauge on the South Wales line. In the opposite direction there were four broad gauge coal trains daily to Swansea, two to London, and one to Neath. London was thus being supplied by both broad and standard gauge coal trains from the same source, the line from Reading to London having become mixed gauge in 1861. This practice lasted only until 1872 when the broad gauge South Wales line was narrowed.

It is interesting also that there were two LNWR trains at this time, one from Aberdare and one from Merthyr, as the LNWR exercised their running powers over the old NAH as far as Hereford where they had joint ownership of the Shrewsbury & Hereford. These trains ran until the late 70s; thereafter the LNWR ran inspection trains twice a year from Tredegar Junction to

Swansea in order to exercise their right, and continued the practice until at least 1909.

Regular traffic appears to have reached a peak of activity around 1885, when nearly 40 coal trains a day moved eastward; of these nine were for the London area, two for the LNWR at Yarnton near Oxford, two for the LSWR at Basingstoke, three for Birkenhead, three for Southampton, twelve for Cardiff by the Rhymney, and four for Newport. In the westward direction, six trains headed for Swansea. There was also an express goods from Manchester to Neath.

By 1899, the number of trains moving eastward had dropped from 40 to 29 a day, the biggest drop being to Cardiff over the Rhymney, reflecting, probably, the exhaustion of the older workings. A further reduction in train movements up to 1913 resulted from increasing the weight of the trains by introducing more powerful locomotives.

GWR 2-8-0 of the 2800 class heads a coal train emerging from Cefn Glas Tunnel in the direction of Quakers Yard. March 1958.

S. Rickard.

8F 2-8-0 heading west through Clarence Street Station. No date.

R. K. Blencowe Coll.

By 1913 a pattern had been established for the long distance haulage of coal into England. From Aberdare, every morning except Sundays, at 00.30 a coal train headed off into the night destined for Yarnton near Oxford, by way of Pontypool Road. An hour later the Bristol goods train followed the same route as far as the Sirhowy valley, where it turned south over the LNWR to re-join the GWR at Newport, thence through the Severn Tunnel. The GWR's new and powerful 2-8-0 freight locomotives of the '2800' class were proved over this route in the early 1900s.

Next away, at 02.30, was the Swindon coal train, this time via Pontypool Road; then there was a pause in eastbound coal traffic until 07.50 when the Salisbury coal train departed, routed down the Sirhowy valley. At Rogerstone near Newport lay a large yard for the marshalling of freight and mineral traffic, though many of the trains from Aberdare went through to their destination. At 14.05 the Southampton train left Aberdare, again heading for Newport and the Severn tunnel. At 18.00 another Yarnton train headed for Pontypool Road, 15 minutes behind a Stoke Gifford train. At 20.30 the Birmingham

train headed for the Sirhowy valley and presumably Gloucester. Another Salisbury train left at 23.00, followed 30 minutes later by the last working of the day for Stoke Gifford. This represented nine regular trains a day from Aberdare, six days a week—over 1 million tons of coal a year. No wonder the class of freight engines developed for hauling coal trains was called the 'Aberdare' class.

While the GWR was moving large quantities of coal from Aberdare eastward into England, the LNWR had developed its access to the port of Cardiff over the track of its ally the Rhymney. Each day nine trains of LNWR empty waggons moved back up from Cardiff by way of the Rhymney valley, joining the Vale of Neath line at Hengoed and as far as Tredegar Junction. Reference to this movement up the Pontypool line is a reminder that all waggons had to be returned when empty, effectively doubling the movements highlighted so far and further adding to the complexity of the arrangements.

There was another significant movement up to Dowlais over the joint GW/RR line from Llancaiach. R.W. Kidner recalls in his revision of D.S.M. Barrie's *The Rhymney Railway* that in this one year, 1913, '400,000 tons of imported ore were dragged and pushed up these heartbreaking grades to feed the hungry furnaces'. This represented two trains in each direction every day between Dowlais and Cardiff, again using the Vale of Neath line between Llancaiach and Penalltau Junction; another five ran over the joint line from Merthyr. The RR also ran three trains from Cwmbach in the Aberdare valley to Cardiff. Elsewhere there was a great variety of general freight movements, for example:

i) stopping goods trains ran daily from Neath to Pontypool Road, from Swansea to Pontypool Rd. and from Swansea to Aberdare, and twice a day from Merthyr via Quakers Yard Low Level to Pontypool Road, and from Aberdare to Pontypool Road,

ii) once a day a train of empties ran from Margam to Aberdare.

iii) a mixed train of goods and empties ran daily from Neath to Mountain Ash.

iv) a daily train carried goods and cattle from Swansea to Aberdare.

v) there was a daily pick-up goods from Neath to Glyn Neath.

vi) four trains a day for Pontypool Road were hauled up the branch from Llanhilleth.

This activity amounted to 100 trains of all types each day in each direction over all or part of the line. As might be expected this traffic increased in wartime. In the First World War 100 trains a week carried steam coal for the Royal Navy in Scotland from Quakers Yard, where they were assembled, through Pontypool Road and on to the West Coast main line. Between August 1914 and December 1918 nearly 5½ million tons of coal was moved along this route alone; in November 1918 nearly 40 extra trains carried 14,000 tons from Quakers Yard in one day on an already busy line.

2-8-0T No. 5237 heading east with a coal train, having just passed Penalltau Junction Box. August 1962.

G. T. Robinson.

With steam to spare 2-6-0 No. 6361 heads towards Aberdare from Mountain Ash. 13 March 1964.
G. T. Robinson.

Since much of the normal traffic on the line was coal for England, it was less affected by the 1926 strike than the main export trade, which lost markets never to be recovered. During the 1930s the volume of traffic remained at about the same level as hitherto, but the pattern of operations changed. Fewer trains travelled directly to their destinations and more coal trains were re-formed at Pontypool Road or Severn Tunnel Junction. In 1935 for instance, there were five long-distance trains, and three for Severn Tunnel Junction, three for Pontypool Road, two for Newport by way of Hall's Road, and one for Cardiff by the old RR line. As a result, drivers spent fewer nights away from home. The Second World War, however, changed matters again, and traffic increased to the two important junctions, although pressure was less than in the First World War as the Navy was no longer burning coal. Nevertheless, typically, in 1942, there were 24 coal trains a day heading for England; most used the line between Aberdare and Sirhowy

Junction, through the single track Quakers Yard tunnel. The traffic was even more concentrated on the difficult section between Quakers Yard and Penalltau Junction, where sharp bends restricted speed to 20 m.p.h. and a succession of junctions presented further impediments. A report in June 1943 stated that during the previous year 37,064 freight trains left south Wales by the Severn Tunnel, the Severn Bridge (Beachley), or Tram-Inn (near Hereford); the week ending 26 July saw a record of 793 trains; in 1943 the weekly average was 750.

There were also restrictions on locomotive weight, especially in the sidings. Much of the land was liable to subsidence and the Crumlin Viaduct had a weight limit. As a concession to the pressures of war, the ban on 4-6-0 type locomotives was lifted for emergencies, though the ban remained total on the 'King' class. In 1943 no more than two locomotives were allowed on the viaduct at a time; tender engines when assisted had to work chimney first, and

7200 class 2-8-2T No. 7221 passes Hirwaun West Box with a train of empty ballast waggons for the nearby Penderyn Quarry. 21 August 1962.

G. T. Robinson.

A west-bound weed-killing train hauled by 2-6-2T No. 4137 passing through Aberdare High Level on 6 June 1963.

R. H. Marrows.

tank engines were not to be coupled to the chimney end of a tender locomotive. By 1963, '7200' class locomotives had also been banned altogether from the viaduct. War conditions, however, caused the ban on the much disliked LMS 0-8-4 tank engines to be lifted, in part at least, as they were permitted between Bird-in-Hand and Ystrad Mynach. The GWR had previously banned them altogether from the former LNWR rights over the line to Cardiff because their long and inflexible wheelbase damaged the track.

Among some of the wartime measures reported by the Newport Divisional Office in 1943 was the provision in July that year of a new staff canteen at Pontypool Road, and stocks of tinned food and biscuits were also to be provided at Pontypool and Aberdare, presumably because of the fear of air-raids and the long working hours. Although parts of south Wales suffered quite severely from air attacks, the Vale of Neath line managed to avoid much damage, though on 31 May 1941 at 02.45 the second waggon of a freight train between Mountain Ash and Middle Duffryn received a direct hit from a German bomb; the driver and fireman were injured, 13 waggons were de-railed and the engine was damaged; both lines were out of use until 10.50.

Most surprisingly, a Service Timetable for Freight Trains for 1 December 1941 'and until further notice' managed to ignore the problems of the war almost completely. No reference was made to 'Black-out', Air-Raid, or emergency precautions, yet the GWR pedigree is apparent with the continued insertion of the instruction that 'Every care must be taken to avoid running over Packs of Hounds, which during the Hunting Season may cross the Line, and all Railway Servants are hereby enjoined to use every care consistent with a due regard being paid to the proper working of the Line and Trains'.

After the war there was a gradual decline, yet despite colliery closures in 1955, three daily long distance trains still worked eastward, and four ran to Pontypool Road., five to Severn Tunnel Junction, and three to Newport, while there were also about six long distance freight trains between west Wales and the Midlands, and there were still four trains a day to Swansea.

Movements of coal into England held up longer than exports, but by 1962, operations were more irregular, though some 100 trains a week still moved eastward, 74 originating in the Aberdare valley, with the remainder being through-freight trains. Of this total of 74, 21 went to the two main junctions, 21 to Newport, and 10 travelled through, but all were destined for England.

If the volume of traffic alone had not been enough to tax the operating management, matters were compounded by the curves, gradients, sections of single line, and multiplicity of junctions. The line was beset with speed restrictions. 15 m.p.h. was normal at the many junctions but five were limited to 5 m.p.h. and on the Crumlin Viaduct it was 8 m.p.h. There were three compulsory stops for goods trains at the top of steep inclines; at Cwm Glyn above Pontypool, at Gelli Tarw above Aberdare, and just below the summit at the top of the Glyn Neath bank. The worst of the gradients were severe by any standards. Heading down the line to Pontypool, goods trains were restricted to 6 m.p.h. for the two miles at 1 in 45. In 1941 42 signal boxes controlled this complex system; just about one a mile. Some were only open during normal working hours but 14 were manned continuously. Sirhowy Junction and Bird-in-Hand West were only a quarter of a mile apart, Hirwaun East and West only 270 yards. The largest gap of 4 miles was between the summit west of Hirwaun, at Hirwaun Pond, and the box at the British Rhondda coal sidings down the Glyn Neath bank. At the other end of the line, Cwm Glyn box was 2½ miles from Pontypool.

LOCOMOTIVES

One of the attractions of the Vale of Neath line was the variety of locomotives found on it, even from the earliest days. Aberdare must have been a fascinating place for lovers of the steam engine, especially in mixed gauge days between 1864 and 1872, when neat little NAH locomotives rubbed shoulders with the broad gauge heavy-weights of the VNR.

NAH LOCOMOTIVES IN CHRONOLOGICAL ORDER				
No	*Wheels*	*Driving Diam.*	*Maker*	*Delivery Notes*
1	0-6-0	5' 3"	E.B.Wilson Nov'54	ex Brassey
2	0-6-0	5' 3"	E.B.Wilson Dec'54	ex Brassey
3	0-6-0	5' 3"	E.B.Wilson Dec'54	ex Brassey
4	0-6-0	5' 3"	E.B.Wilson Jan'55	ex Brassey
20	0-4-2	4' 6"	Dodds &Co Dec'54	ex Brassey later 0-4-2ST
21	0-4-2	4' 6"	Dodds &Co Dec'54	ex Brassey later 0-4-0ST
22	0-4-2	4' 6"	Dodds &Co Dec'54	ex Brassey later 0-4-2T
5	0-6-0	5' 3"	E.B.Wilson 1855	
6	0-6-0	5' 3"	E.B.Wilson 1855	
10	0-6-0	5' 3"	E.B.Wilson 1855	
27	2-4-0	6' 0"	E.B.Wilson 1855	'Antelope'
28	2-4-0	6' 0"	E.B.Wilson 1855	'Reindeer'
29	2-4-0	6' 0"	E.B.Wilson 1855	'Elk'
30	2-4-0	6' 0"	E.B.Wilson Aug'56	'Gazelle'
7	0-6-0T	5' 3"	E.B.Wilson 1856	
8	0-6-0T	5' 3"	E.B.Wilson 1856	
9	0-6-0	5' 0"	E.B.Wilson 1856	
11	,,	,,	,, 1856	
12	,,	,,	" Jan'57	boiler burst, Nantyderry
13	,,	,,	" Jan'57	
14	,,	,,	,, 1858	
15	,,	,,	,,	
16	,,	,,	,,	
17	,,	,,	,,	
18	,,	,,	,,	
19	,,	,,	,,	

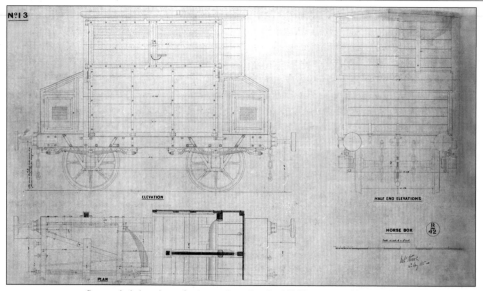

Sturrocks' drawing of a horse-box for the NAH, prepared in 1855.

WIMM.

NEWPORT, ABERGAVENNY AND HEREFORD RAILWAY

The agreements made between the NAH and the LNWR included provision that the LNWR would operate the line and supply the locomotives. It was LNWR policy, as far as their railways along the Welsh marches were concerned, to engage Thomas Brassey as locomotive contractor, and so, when the LNWR terminated the arrangement with the NAH in September 1854, it was to Brassey the NAH turned. He supplied the first 7 locomotives, four 0-6-0s made by E.B. Wilson and three 0-4-2s by Dodds & Co.. A further batch of three of the 0-6-0s followed. Thereafter the company relied for goods engines on further batches of ten 0-6-0s with slightly smaller driving wheels, and for passenger engines on four 2-4-0s, the only NAH locomotives to receive names. The only other type, unusually for this company, was a double-framed tank engine; these well- and back-tanks earned the name 'Duck-back tanks'. They were first used on the Llanhilleth branch and were later moved to Pontypool for banking coal trains up to Abergavenny and Llanfihangel. There are few other clues as to which of these engines worked over the TVE; the later 0-6-0s coincided with the opening in 1858 and, according to E.L. Ahrons, the 2-4-0s were mainly based at Worcester after the formation of the West Midland. All the NAH locomotives passed into GWR ownership but most were withdrawn during the 1870s; only the 2-4-0s survived until the end of the century. 'Reindeer' spent time on the Severn Valley line, with 'Elk' being the last to go in 1903.

VALE OF NEATH RAILWAY

The 25 locomotives of the VNR were all built as tank engines, and whereas the NAH operated fairly standard designs with no special problems to generate controversy, the VNR, owing to the nature of its terrain and being laid to the broad gauge, experienced high costs of both track and locomotive maintenance, which led to criticism of the weight of some of its engines. When T.E. Harrison made his report to the Committee of Investigation in 1859, he said that three of the engines each weighed 50 tons. Owing to the absence of compensating levers, these could place up to 20 tons on one axle and should be converted to tender engines, so that the maximum weight on any axle could be only 13 tons. His report said, 'This is a crushing weight and far beyond anything with which I am acquainted. I have no hesitation therefore in stating that the weight of these engines must prove destructive to your permanent way'.

The first group of locomotives, delivered between October and the end of 1851 and numbered 1-6, were six 4-4-0 saddle tanks, designed by Gooch & Co. and built by Robert Stephenson; they resembled classes in use on other contemporary railways such as the GWR and the South Devon. With 5' 6' driving wheels they were allocated mainly to passenger trains, though they also hauled mineral trains when this trade started. Their delivery was late and for the first few months the VNR had to hire 0-6-0 goods locomotives from the GWR.

In the second half of 1854, a further six locomotives were delivered, three 4-4-0STs but with smaller driving wheels and larger cylinders, (numbered 7, 8, and 9), and three 0-6-0STs from the Vulcan Foundry with 4' 9' driving wheels (numbered 10, 11, and 12). The later 4-4-0s proved heavy on maintenance and in 1858 No.8 was converted to 0-6-0ST. This batch of six locomotives met the increased demand following the opening of the Merthyr line and the extension to the Canal Head, and were also intended for the Dare and Aman branches, where numbers 7 and 9 were normally employed, while 8, 10, 11, and 12 were engaged on general main line mineral traffic.

This was sufficient capacity until the completion of the extension to Middle Duffryn in November 1856, when three further 0-6-0STs, numbers 13, 14, and 15, were added. These engines worked mainly on the Glyn Neath bank and were the subject of Harrison's forthright criticism due to their great weight which was attributable to their large 18' cylinders and 1,500 gallon water capacity, as opposed to the usual 900. By 1861 all three had been converted to tender engines, the first having demonstrated the validity of Harrison's advice.

The 0-6-0 saddle tanks were so successful at

VALE OF NEATH LOCOMOTIVES IN CHRONOLOGICAL ORDER

No	Year Built	Wheel Arrang't	Driving WheelDiam	Builder*	Conversion Year	Wheel Arrang't
Broad Gauge						
1	Oct'51	4-4-0ST	5' 6'	R.S.		
2	"	"	"	"		
3	"	"	"	"		
4	"	"	"	"		
5	"	"	"	"		
6	"	"	"	"		
7	Jun'54	4-4-0ST	5' 0"	R.S.	1860	0-6-0ST
8	Aug'54	4-4-0ST	5' 0"	R.S.	1858	0-6-0ST
9	Oct'54	4-4-0ST	5' 0"	R.S.	1860	0-6-0ST
10	Sep'54	0-6-0ST	4' 9"	VF		
11	Oct'54	0-6-0ST	4' 9"	VF		
12	Oct'54	0-6-0ST	4' 9"	VF		
13	Dec'56	0-6-0ST	4' 9"	VF	1860	0-6-0
14	Dec'56	0-6-0ST	4' 9"	VF	1861	0-6-0
15	Jan'57	0-6-0ST	4' 9"	VF	1861	0-6-0
16	Nov'61	0-6-0ST	4' 6"	SG		
17	Nov'61	0-6-0ST	4' 6"	SG		
18	Dec'61	0-6-0ST	4' 6"	SG		
19	Dec'61	0-6-0ST	4' 6"	SG		
Standard Gauge						
20	Apr'64	0-6-0ST	5' 2"	R.S.		
21	May'64	0-6-0ST	5' 2"	R.S.		
22	Dec'64	0-8-0T	4' 6"	SG		
23	Dec'64	0-8-0T	4' 6"	SG		
24	Mar'65	0-6-0ST	4' 6"	VF		
25	Mar'65	0-6-0ST	4' 6"	VF		

*R.S.—R. Stephenson; VF—Vulcan Foundry; SG— Slaughter Gruning.

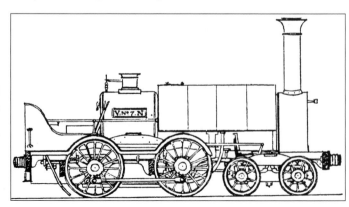

Vale of Neath Railway 4-4-0T Nos. 7-9 series. Built by R. Stephenson & Co., 1854.
  Based on a drawing by RAS Abbott.

handling the coal traffic that a further four, numbers 16-19, were added at the end of 1861, with slightly smaller cylinders and only 4' 6' driving wheels. These were the last broad gauge locomotives built for the VNR as standard gauge coal traffic began on 27 February 1864. As had been the case at the outset, the company found itself without any suitable locomotives and this time hired them from the LNWR. However in April and May 1864 two standard gauge 0-6-0STs were delivered, followed in March 1865 by a further pair. They all had double frames, the second pair having outside cylinders and smaller driving wheels. Also in December 1864 were delivered two controversial 0-8-0Ts, which Joshua Williams had seen as the solution to reconciling power with axle loading. These were the first of the type on a main line railway in Britain, although followed shortly by similar locomotives from the same supplier, Slaughter Grunig, for the Great Northern.

WEST MIDLAND RAILWAY, GWR, and BRITISH RAIL

There is no evidence that any of the locomotives built by the West MR were used on the TVE; on the contrary it seems that they were mainly confined to the former OWW area. No doubt there were exceptions but no examples have come to light. It therefore seems likely that the NAH locomotives continued to be used until they were replaced by new GWR examples. The broad gauge operation of the former VNR continued largely unaltered until 1872 when the third rail was removed from both the VNR and SWR lines, and the VNR locomotives were withdrawn or dispersed to areas where the broad gauge continued. However after the opening of the link at Middle Duffryn and absorption of the West MR and VNR into the Great Western, traffic growth called for additional motive power and the GWR introduced 15 of a new class of 0-6-0 tender goods engines which were housed at Pontypool Road to handle coal traffic. In 1867 these engines were replaced with 0-6-0STs of the '1016' class, and by the early '70s, this class dominated the coal movements on the Neath to Pontypool line, and most of the through passenger traffic as well. They were so successful that between 1870 and 1881, 266 of a basically similar pattern, known as the '1076' class, were built at Swindon. Seventeen of them

0-6-0ST No.1044 at Aberdare. Date unknown.
Cynon Valley Borough Libraries.

'Aberdare' class 2-6-0 No. 2620, when new.

WIMM: GW Coll.

In the Vale of Neath, 2-8-0 No 3860 hauls a west-bound mixed freight near Melyncourt Halt. 16 March 1964.

G. T. Robinson.

were still allocated to Aberdare in 1902 and one was still there during the Second World War.

Monthly records of GWR locomotive allocations from 1902 present a picture of the types of locomotive employed on the line from Neath to Pontypool Road. Three sheds were relevant: Neath, Aberdare, and Pontypool Road itself; there was a fourth at Glyn Neath but this was only for banking engines. Of course not all the locomotives at either Neath or Pontypool

Road were for employment on the cross-country line, but it is possible to draw some conclusions and perceive trends.

E.L. Ahrons writing about the train operations of the last part of the nineteenth century noted with interest that the GWR used 0-6-0 saddle tank engines for hauling Aberdare coal trains all the way to Swindon. With a strictly limited capacity of only 1,040 gallons of water, frequent stops were necessary. The length of the trains was obviously limited by the power of these tough but small locomotives, but they nevertheless dominated the coal movements on and off the Vale of Neath line for some thirty years. By 1902 Pontypool Road still had about 30 saddle tanks but these were now augmented by over 40 of William Dean's 0-6-0 tender engines. Some 10 of Armstrong's 0-6-0 tender engines appeared at Aberdare and 9 Dean Goods 0-6-0s, but, such was the intensity if the traffic, something larger was urgently needed.

The first trial of a new engine involved William Dean's (and the GW's) first 4-6-0, No. 36, on coal trains between Newport and Swindon. Built in 1896, it was a 4-6-0 tender engine with double frames and 4' 6" driving wheels and was nicknamed 'the Crocodile'. It was not a success and was withdrawn in 1905. In 1899 the so called 'Kruger' class was introduced; the first example (No. 2601) was also a double-framed 4-6-0, but it was an ungainly machine and suffered visually from having a large saddle sandbox set between the chimney and the safety valve on the domeless boiler. This was no great success either and an adaptation, No. 2602, was eventually built in 1901 as a 2-6-0. It made a brief appearance on the Vale of Neath line, being housed at Aberdare, and eight more of the class were built, but again they were not entirely successful and all were withdrawn by 1907, replaced finally by the 'Aberdare' class. The first of these 2-6-0s, No. 33, appeared in 1900, to be followed by 40 more by February 1902. Initially it had been intended to use these larger locomotives on coal trains from Newport, picking up from Rogerstone yard, but by the end of 1901, ten had allocated to Aberdare shed for hauling trains direct from source. By 1903, 17 of the class were at Aberdare.

Meanwhile further developments in goods locomotives had been taking place, as part of Churchward's continuing effort to produce a limited number of standard classes, exploiting interchangeable parts as far as possible. No. 97, the pioneer 2-8-0, was tested on coal trains and, on 12 December 1904, Churchward reported that it was doing well on these trains between Stoke Gifford and Paddington, hauling 60 waggons and a brake van weighing 920 tons in all. It could have taken even heavier loads but the facilities could only cope with 35 waggon trains. The 'Aberdares' had been an undoubted improvement over the saddle tanks but the new locomotives were better still, being more powerful, reliable in service and cheaper to maintain. The first allocation of three locomotives of what became the '2800' class appeared at Aberdare shed in 1906, No. 97 itself being among them. The new locomotives did not oust the 'Aberdares' from the line for many years, as the following table listing allocations to Pontypool Road and Aberdare sheds clearly shows:

Year	A'DARE		PPRD	
	'A'dares'	2800s	'A'dares'	2800s
1906	14	3	-	-
1908	8	6	14	-
1913	14	6	11	1
1916	8	7	15	25
1920	10	11	15	20
1923	10	17	15	12
1928	5	13	5	10
1937	1	9	1	7
1943	1	12	5	1
1948	-	12	1	5
1957	-	7	-	6
1963	-	9	-	6

Other types of freight locomotive then followed; the '4200' class 2-8-0T, built especially for the congested lines of south Wales, appeared at Neath in 1916, and thereafter these locomotives were to be seen at all four sheds. Neath tended to have the larger number, and three or four were normally based at Glyn Neath for banking. They were a particularly robust class and able to cope with the tight curves in south Wales without seriously damaging the

2-8-0Ts 4275 and 4281 at Glyn Neath Shed. October 1959.
F. K. Davies.

R.O.D. 2-8-0 No. 3049 at Pontypool Road shed. 5 September 1937.
F. K. Davies.

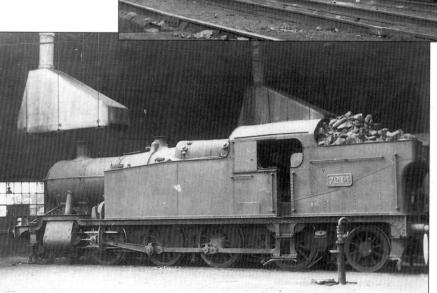

The size of the coal bunker of a 7200 class 2-8-2T is emphasised in this photograph taken in Aberdare Shed in May 1951.
H. C. Casserley.

track; one of these still surviving in preservation, No. 5239, was based at Neath from the mid-thirties to the early sixties. The GWR in fact built too many of them for the declining traffic and, after time in store, the surplus locomotives were converted to the 2-8-2T wheel arrangement, which permitted a larger coal bunker, thus increasing their range. The coal bunker was as large as many tenders and, as the '7200' class, they appeared at Aberdare in the late 1930s; Pontypool Road had eight of them right up to the end. The R.O.D. standard 2-8-0s of Great Central design appeared in the late '20s and, by the middle of the Second World War, Pontypool Road had ten of them. At this time also, American 2-8-0s supplemented the GW locomotives before seeing service in Europe; ten were at Pontypool Road, six at Neath and, for a short time in 1943, a few found themselves at Aberdare. After the war, Pontypool Road had an austerity 2-8-0 and then in the late '50s the British Rail 2-10-0s, but the latter would not have ventured on the Vale of Neath line. Stanier 8Fs did however regularly penetrate as far as Aberdare.

In later years class 8F 2-8-0s augmented the stock of locomotives. On 13 March 1964 No. 48450 was engaged on a west-bound mixed freight, here seen approaching Cresselley Crossing. *G. T. Robinson.*

8F 2-8-0 No. 48470 takes water on the relief line for north-bound trains at Pontypool Road. September 1963.
F. K. Davies.

0-4-2T No. 1471 in the lifting shop at Aberdare. May 1951.
H. C. Casserley.

0-6-0PT No. 2781 and guard's van at Merthyr, 17 June 1937.
F. K. Davies.

GWR No. 65 started life in 1914 as Rhymney Railway No. 25. Built originally by Hudswell Clarke, it was fitted with a taper boiler in 1931, and survived until 1954. It was stablemate at Aberdare with another of its class, No. 63.
H. C. Casserley.

5600 class locomotive at Glyn Neath outside the single road shed, principally for banking engines. June 1963.
R. H. Marrows.

0-6-0PT No. 4632 takes water at Hirwaun en route to Pontypool Road in 1951.
F. K. Davies.

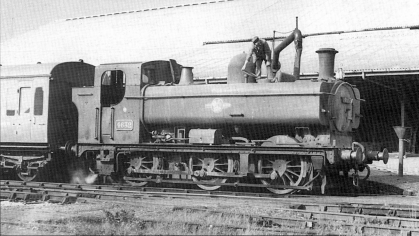

0-6-0PT No. 7773 and guard's van shunt in the Brickyard Sidings at Hirwaun prior to assembling a train, in 1951.
F. K. Davies.

Passenger locomotives on the line had seen less change; two 2-4-0T 'metro' tanks were based at Aberdare from 1899, and in 1902 Aberdare, rather surprisingly, had two 'Bulldog' 4-4-0s, 'Laira' and 'Sir Stafford', besides the oddity No. 3552, (a broad gauge 0-4-4T converted in 1900 to a standard gauge 4-4-0 tender engine). The biggest change came in 1906 when steam rail-cars, referred to by the Great Western as Steam Rail-Motors (SRM), appeared for the first time on the main line and on the then busy Cwmaman branch near Aberdare where two cars were generally in use at one time. Because overhaul was needed more frequently than for locomotives, a large number (Nos 1, 2, 3, 5, 7, and 8) appeared in the period leading up to the war, followed by Nos. 13, 17, and 90 and, in the '20s, Nos. 38, 54 and 67.

Shortly before the First World War, further changes took place, notably 2-4-2Ts of the '3600' class and, exceptionally in 1919 and until 1921, a 'Duke' class 4-4-0 No. 3284 'Isle of Jersey'. Steam rail-car services ceased in the late 1920s and were replaced by auto-trains, initially worked by ancient 0-6-0T engines, and later by the purpose-built '5400'/'6400' class from 1932. Number 6400 itself was based at Pontypool Road for nearly the whole of its existence, from December 1937 until January 1963.

During the 1920s, 0-6-2Ts began to appear from some of the absorbed south Wales railways. This had been a particularly successful type of locomotive on both the Taff Vale and the Rhymney, and by 1928 Aberdare had eight of them. When in 1924 the GWR introduced its own design—the '5600' class—five or six were stationed at Aberdare and Pontypool Road and the class was represented there right to the end of steam. These, together with a small number of '4500' class 2-6-2Ts, and the pannier tanks of classes '5700' and '6400' hauled most of the passenger trains on the line. One notable visitor was the sole '4600' class 4-4-2T, No. 4600, which started its brief career in south Wales in 1913 and returned to Neath from Birmingham in 1923 before being broken up in 1925.

No. 2975 'Lord Palmer', one of Churchward's straight-framed 'Saints', stands on the relief line at Pontypool Road, facing north. ca. 1936.

V. R. Webster.

At the south end of Pontypool Road Station, 0-6-0PT No. 9650 arrives with the 11.07 a.m. from Neath while 'County' class No. 1020 'County of Monmouth' awaits departure with the 9.05 a.m. Liverpool to Plymouth express. 16 April 1963.

R. H. Marrows.

Pontypool Road, because of its location on a main line and as an important marshalling point for freight trains, saw a great variety of locomotive types over the years. Back in 1908 it had a 'Duke' and three 'Bulldogs'; during the First World War the 'Bulldogs' were joined by a 'Badminton' and by 1923 it had three 'County' class 4-4-0s, an 'Atbara', a 'Flower' and five 'Saints'. The maximum number of locomotives based there was over 100 during the First and Second World Wars. After the intense activity of the Second World War, when Pontypool Road boasted some 18 different classes of locomotive, including its own stable of 'Granges', 'Halls', and '4300' class 2-6-0s, no fewer than twelve GWR classes were still represented in 1957, as well as ex-LMS 0-8-0s (5) and 2-8-0s (3). Even as late as 1963 the allocation comprised:

6	'2800's
21	pannier tanks
9	'Halls'
2	large 2-6-2Ts
3	'4300's
7	'5600's
12	'Granges'
8	'7200's

Neath, too, attracted an interesting variety of locomotives over the years. A plethora of small saddle and pannier tanks were most evident at the turn of the century and still formed the backbone of the depot's allocation in 1921, supplemented by four Dean Goods, one 'Aberdare', six R.O.D.s, six '4300's, a 'Bulldog'—No 3338 'Swift'—and SRM No. 82.

By 1934 pannier tanks began to dominate the local work as saddle tanks were gradually withdrawn or converted. The number of Dean Goods was also reduced, but the '2800' 2-8-0s were now represented although No. 6680 was the only member of the '5600' class at the depot. The SRM was now No. 70. Just prior to nationalisation only two saddle tanks survived— Nos 1715 and 2192—the pannier tanks having taken their place. No. 3455 'Starling' was the only 'Bulldog', but 2-8-0Ts were well represented with no fewer than 10 examples, including the ever-present 5239. There was still only one GW 0-6-2T, but No. 6613 and Collett 2-6-2T No. 8104 would both surely have visited the Vale of Neath line on a regular basis. By 1963, with steam rapidly approaching its demise,

the Neath allocation boasted five 'Castles', three 'Halls' and a 'Grange', though these would have seen greater use on the South Wales main line.

The physical nature of the Vale of Neath line with its curves and gradients, the density of the heavy coal traffic, and the frequent stops on the passenger services obviously influenced the locomotive types used and precluded the more glamorous express passenger engines. Except for the through coal trains to England, tank engines prevailed and more than held their own. In the nineteenth century the typical locomotive was undoubtedly the ubiquitous 0-6-0 saddle tank; in the 20th, it was the 'Aberdare', the '2800' and '4200' for freight, with the '5600' being useful for both passenger and mineral traffic.

2-6-0 No. 6361 running into Hirwaun with the 2.25 p.m. from Pontypool Road to Neath on 11 April 1955.
R. M. Casserley.

A shining 'Grange' class 4-6-0 No. 6810 'Blakemere Grange' hauls a mixed eastbound freight through Hengoed High Level. No date.   *R. E. Toop.*

4-6-0 'Hall' class No. 6928 'Underley Hall' heads a north-bound express beneath an unsettled sky at Pontypool Road. May 1963.

John Davies.

Stanier 'Jubilee' 4-6-0 No. 45577 'Bengal' heads a south-bound express at Pontypool Road. A BR standard Mk. 1 coach, in the characteristic chocolate and cream livery intended for named expresses, stands in the Vale of Neath bay—further evidence of the variety of coaching stock engaged on the line. April 1963.

John Davies.

Chapter 6

EPILOGUE

Two hundred years later Gilpin and Russel Wallace would find the Valley of the Neath much as they left it, even though the railway which came after them is still there. Now it is only single track, and winds its way from Riverside to Glyn Neath through thick woodland to the surviving open-cast mine. The valley is green, the air clear, and the hillsides full of colour at all seasons of the year. The people who ran the old railway and the intermediate stations have gone, but the viaduct and aqueduct survive at Aberdulais, together with Llewellyn's cutting; and the Clydach Brook still flows over Brunel's wrought iron bridge at Resolven. The lower part of the Glyn Neath bank is lost in the dense tree growth on the steep hillside and is obscured from the highway, but Pontwalby viaduct stands silent in the damp and eerie woodland. Further up, the bank has been severed by the main road, and the Pencaedrain tunnel is fast disappearing under earthworks, though to the left of the highway the steep and picturesque valley east of the tunnel can still be found, with the ledge which carried the railway clearly visible. Little remains of Hirwaun station site, but Gelli Tarw Junction is quite recognisable near the farm whose name it borrowed, and a single line of track from the Tower Colliery still runs down the long slope towards Aberdare. Here, the sole surviving station on the line has recently been restored, though, perversely, not as a railway station; the modern railway prefers a bus shelter on the opposite platform for the passenger train service down the valley, along the old Taff Vale line.

The enduring picturesque I: Riverside in 1993.

GBJ.

The enduring picturesque II: Cefn Glas Tunnel, east portal 1993.

DD.

Station staff at Quakers Yard High Level early in the 20th century.
R. W. Kidner Coll.

Pannier tank No. 9600 survives at the Birmingham Railway Museum, but only a single track of railway now remains beneath the foot-bridge at Gadlys, Aberdare. Photographed in 1964.
GBJ.

Five anonymous stalwarts of Pontypool Road.
GBJ. Coll.

The Cynon valley railways, with all their intricate connections and intense industrial activity, had their share of railway characters, some of whom survive in 1996 to recall anecdotes and experiences. Walter Stimpson, more usually known as 'Stimp', a carriage and waggon examiner at Aberdare and an acknowledged authority on time-tables, had a habit of appearing on the platform where he would delight in asking passengers their destination and then telling them, from memory, where to change, complete with departure times and appropriate platforms. Alf Moon, a signalman at Middle Duffryn box, was another with a prodigious memory, but in his case it covered the names of the men on all the shifts in every department on the railway. Being a frugal type, he once stuffed grass in a punctured bicycle tyre until he could find a replacement. During the 1940s the Goods Traffic Inspector at Aberdare High Level was a former Manchester and Milford man from Strata Florida. With waxed ginger moustache and walking stick to support legs which suffered from gout, he was a colourful character. Welsh was his native tongue and his English was inclined to be a literal translation. Shortly after his arrival he asked a shunter, 'Those trucks, who belongs to them?' Henceforth he was known as 'Rees Trucks'.

The view looking north from the former down platform at Aberdare; in 1995 this was the only intermediate platform on the Vale of Neath line still in use. The recently carefully restored station building on the former up platform, standing vacant at the time of writing, bears silent testimony to the oddly blinkered vision of modern managements. Pacer No. 143605 formed the 13.45 Barry Island to Aberdare service on 1 August 1995.
Neil Sprinks.

An undated photograph showing the view in the opposite direction to that portrayed above.
NMRW.

Engine and van, with guard Ken Davies of Aberdare, arrive at Mountain Ash to pick up a train. May 1964. *GBJ.*

Driver George Bower pauses during shunting at Cresselley Crossing. 13 March 1964. *G. T. Robinson.*

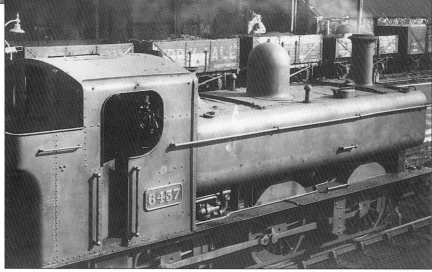

A signalman's view of No. 6437 at Hirwaun, 1951. *F. K. Davies.*

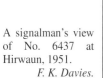

A shunter at Cresselley crossing, Mountain Ash, was another eccentric. He was reputed to have damaged his foot deliberately, with the help of a moving waggon, in order to be able to claim compensation, and is reputed to have left £80,000 to a boys' home. Many railwaymen supplemented their income as and when they could. Some signalmen took advantage of intervals between trains; one was a barber, others were shoe or watch repairers. Tony Pook of Hirwaun was a part-time window cleaner and kept his ladder and trolley under his signal box.

The transformation of the Cynon valley from industrial bedlam to rural tranquillity is not yet complete, but the dramatic progress so far has effectively removed most of the traces of the TVE. The historic Middle Duffryn is now no more than a straight stretch of main road, and an extravagant piece of road-straightening recently removed most of the remnants of Penrhiwceiber High Level. The Cefn Glas tunnel still hides in the trees on the steep slope of the mountain and its eastern portal is readily visible from a lay-by on the A 470. Quakers Yard High Level and its viaducts have gone, though abutments are still discernable, especially in winter. The line can be traced through Edwardsville to the site of Treharris station, now a playground. The houses here are, nearly all, still prone to subsidence; no wonder the railway viaducts had to be shored up.

Treharris had its moment of fame in 1958 when the Duke of Edinburgh's train terminated there. This was because the preferred terminus at Nelson and Llancaiach was located close to the boundary between three local authorities, which would have caused an inconvenient amount of complex protocol. L.M. Whiteman, the lampman at Penalltau at the time, has recalled that a trial run was made, a week before, with a pristine 'Castle' class locomotive from Cardiff, up the Rhymney to Penalltau; not a wisp of excess smoke emerged from a fire only four inches thick burning the very best Welsh coal.

By September 1964, Aberdare Shed was already looking sparse; Nos. 5237 (l.) and 4259 (r.) are the identifiable locomotives in this view. 7 September 1964.

GBJ.

On 7 September 1964, Shedmaster
Howard Jones supervised a removal for
scrapping by No. 3610.

GBJ.

By June 1967, Aberdare Shed was derelict.
GBJ.

A rare event at Treharris; 'Castle' class No. 5074 'Hampden' after arrival with H.R.H. the Duke of Edinburgh. 25 July 1958.

WIMM: GW Coll.

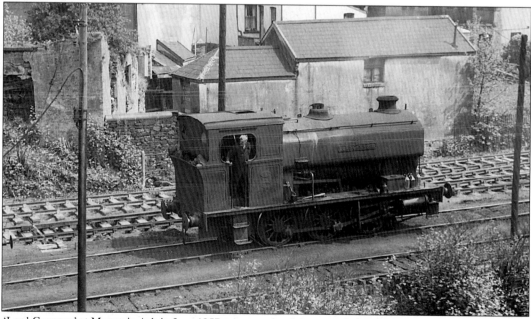

'Lord Camrose' at Mountain Ash in June 1957, an example of the many industrial locomotives which indirectly served the Vale of Neath line.

GBJ.

Trelewis Halt 24 April 1964, Arrival from the west. *Alan Jarvis*

Trelewis Halt 24 April 1964, Departure westward. *Alan Jarvis*

Beyond Treharris the track is still laid, though derelict, past the junctions to the collieries, winding round the site of Trelewis Halt to the bare rough grass which used to be Nelson and Llancaiach. This is where another remnant of operating railway, the former joint GW/Rhymney line, still moves coal from Taff Merthyr along to Penalltau and down the old Rhymney main line which still carries passengers. Although Hengoed Low Level survives, the site of High Level is covered in a particularly thick crop of bushes and small trees, right up to the viaduct, which still stands. Beyond is an area where extensive road improvement has obliterated traces of the railway; the Bryn tunnel is buried and Bird-In-Hand Junction is a housing estate, though the site of Pontllanfraith Low Level station is recognisable with the help of a small chapel which serves as a marker. Past Penar, the track is a wilderness in a cutting. The site of Crumlin High level is still identifiable but, as with Clarence Street, all the buildings have gone, so there are no Liddell stations left on the line. It was from the signalman at Crumlin High Level that Driver Rupert Davies heard a shout as he took his '2800' class locomotive eastward at the head of a train of marine mines, two to a waggon, packed in straw to minimise disturbance; 'Rupert, your first waggon's on fire'. It was dark—the darkness of wartime—and the train was about to embark on the Crumlin Viaduct; Rupert grabbed a bucket from the footplate, clambered over the coal in the tender, and as the locomotive lurched and rolled 200 feet above the valley, flipped open the water tank cover and lowered his bucket on a rope; fortunately the tank was fairly full and he was able to throw enough water onto the flames to avert disaster. The last of the job was done with the help of the water column at Crumlin Junction.

A view from the road bridge at Nelson and Llancaiach showing the GW/RR Joint line to Dowlais (Cae Harris) climbing away to the right from the Vale of Neath line. The train is the 4.15 p.m. from Dowlais to Ystrad Mynach, headed by No. 5634, on 13 March 1964.   *G. T. Robinson.*

The same vantage point in 1994.   *GBJ.*

No. 3440 'City of Truro' and No. 4358 work an Ian Allan Railtour up the Glyn Valley on 16 May 1957.
John Hodge.

'City of Truro' is detached at Crumlin Junction to preceed the train across the viaduct. 16 May 1957.
John Hodge.

Perhaps the most dramatic change has come about in the Glyn Valley as it winds its way down to Pontypool; Coxe would again recognise the steep valley sides, the impressive height of the mountain, and the tree-covered slopes. Now a considerable mental effort is required to conjure up the images of glistening, newly mined coal in rusty drams or waggons, with rain-washed slurry everywhere underfoot, or a thin sun shining through coal dust thick as fog. Harsh as they were, even these images may have been picturesque, provided the observer was not encumbered by a pick and a miner's lamp.

Pontypool Road is also transformed, but there is something tragic about the pathetic rump of a station that is left and the flattened site of the great engine shed, now occupied by a fast food shop and a petrol station. Gone is that windy, busy place with its frequent roar of trains and milling crowds of people, some looking for a seat in over-crowded carriages, others pushing into the smokey, steamy buffet, struggling with too much luggage; while, on the massive sidings, the clatter and jangle of moving waggons bore constant testimony to the main activity of what was once a very important junction.

Clarence Street Station shortly before demolition. No date.
Torfaen Museum, Pontypool.

Welsh wet day on the Crumlin viaduct, September 1958.
V. R. Webster.

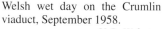

A once familiar sight at Hirwaun as the banker waits to follow the passenger train down to Aberdare. May 1964.

Alan Jarvis.

In May 1964 it was still possible to experience the variety and complexity of the Vale of Neath line. Here an east-bound train passes the High Level coal sidings, as it approaches Quakers Yard East Junction.

Alan Jarvis.

A bright spring morning at Quakers Yard, in May 1964, gives no hint of the impending withdrawal of passenger services, as No. 9488 takes the 11.00 a.m. from Aberdare towards Pontypool Road.

Alan Jarvis.

The closed Booking Hall at Pontypool Road, just before demolition. 1993.

GBJ.

The station master's house of old Pontypool Road station photographed in 1995.

DD.

Gelli Tarw in 1994.

DD.

Trelewis and in the distance the site of the collieries. 1993.

DD.

BIBLIOGRAPHY

AHRONS, E.L., *Locomotive and Train Working, South Wales.* Heffer.

BARRIE, D.S.M., *South Wales, Regional Railway History.* D&C. (1980).

BYLES, Aubrey, *History of the Monmouthshire Railway and Canal Co.* (1982).

COOKE, R.A., *Track Layout Diagrams.*

COXE W.. *Tour in Monmouthshire.* (1801).

DAVIES, W.L., *The Bridges of Merthyr Tydvil.* Glamorgan R.O. (1992).

DYOS, H.J. & ALDCROFT, D.H., *British Transport.* Pelican.

ELTON, A., *British Railways.* Collins.

EVANS, E.A., *Three Viaducts.*

EVANS, E.A., *Rails to Nelson.*

GILPIN, William, *Observations on the River Wye and several parts of South Wales.* 1770.

GLADWIN, D.D.& J.M., *The Canals of the Welsh Valleys.* Oakwood.

HAMILTON ELLIS, C., *Railway Carriages in the British Isles.* Allen & Unwin

HARESNAPE, B. & SWAIN, A., *Churchward Locomotives.* Ian Allan.

JONES, G.E., *Modern Wales* 1485-1979. Cambridge.

KIDNER, R.W, *The Rhymney Railway.* The Oakwood Press.

MacDERMOT, E.T., *History of the Great Western Railway.* Ian Allan.

History of Technology, vol. XI. Mansell Publishing, (1986.)

MAYNARD, Henry, *Handbook to the Crumlin Viaduct.* (1862).

MEAR, J.F,. *The Story of Cwmdare.* (1991).

Murray's Handbook for Travellers in South Wales (1877 ed.) *Route 10.*

NOCK, O.S., *GWR. in the Twentieth Century.* Ian Allan.

PAGE, J., *Forgotten Railways, South Wales.* D & C.

PHILLIPS, Olive, *Monmouthshire, A County History.* R. Hale.

POLLINS, H., *Britain's Railways, An Industrial History.* D&C.

PRITCHARD, A.J., *Railways of S.E. Monmouthshire.*

Railway Magazine, July & August (1956). T.B. Sands.

Railway Magazine, September (1957) .

Railway Magazine, January (1910.) H. Rake.

R.C.& T.S. *The Locomotives of the GWR.*

SIMMONS, Prof., *Railways, An Anthology.* (1991).

SIMMONS, Prof., *The Victorian Railway.* Thames & Hudson. (1991).

TUPLIN, W.A. *GWR Steam.* Allen & Unwin.

TUPLIN, W.A. *Saints and Sinners.* Allen & Unwin.

The VNR initials etched in a window at Neath Riverside.

Bob Grant Coll.

INDEX